Out of the Wilderness

Out of the Wilderness

The Life of Abraham Lincoln

WILLIAM HANCHETT

UNIVERSITY OF ILLINOIS PRESS
Urbana and Chicago

This book is printed on acid-free paper.

Library of Congress Cataloging-in-Publication Data

Hanchett, William. 1922–
    Out of the wilderness : the life of Abraham Lincoln / William
Hanchett.
        p.   cm.
    ISBN 978-0-252-02111-4. — ISBN 978-0-252-06400-5 (pbk.)
    1. Lincoln, Abraham, 1809–1865. 2. Presidents—United States—
Biography. I. Title.
E457.H237 1994
973.7'092—dc20
    [B]   93-39609
                                                                        CIP

To Angie and Colin

Contents

Preface

In the preface to his popular 1952 biography of Abraham Lincoln, Benjamin P. Thomas noted that although many books had been written about Lincoln a major need, "perhaps *the* major need so far as most persons are concerned," remained unfulfilled. There was, said Thomas, no readable, reliable, and reasonably short biography by which general readers and high school and college students with limited time could be introduced to Lincoln.

In the midtwentieth century Thomas's *Abraham Lincoln* admirably fulfilled its objective, but it is dated now and today not many people have the time or inclination to read its 550 pages. For this and other reasons, far too many Americans have lost all meaningful contact with Lincoln. They do not know him as a man—a husband, a father, a friend—and they have only the vaguest notion of the problems he faced as president. They do not understand how the experiences of his boyhood and young manhood awakened his intelligence and helped shape his character. They do not appreciate that hard study and clear thinking offset his lack of formal education and enabled him to become one of the foremost attorneys of his state. They do not realize that his devotion to the Declaration of Independence's promise of ultimate equality for all caused him to take the uncompromising stand against the spread of slavery that led to the secession of the Southern states and to the Civil War. They do not understand that not only was the nation of which he was president divided into warring sections, the section he led was itself divided by powerful and hostile interests and that, as a consequence, the North's victory over the South required a near-miracle of balanced political leadership. They do not know that his emancipation of slaves was the most controversial act of his controversial presidency. Most regrettable of all, they do not realize that he fought to keep the Union together, not for its own sake, but in order to preserve the American experiment in democracy, so that government of the people, by the people, and for the people would not perish from the earth. In short, ignorance of Lincoln and of his place in American and world history is widespread. A new introductory biography is more urgently needed than ever before.

The contrast in length and comprehensiveness between Thomas's *Abraham Lincoln* and this book is a reflection of a generational difference in which it is difficult to take any satisfaction. Yet we must recognize that history is being more broadly conceived and written today than in the past and that even a leader of Lincoln's stature faces stiff competition for the attention of readers. Under these circumstances, brevity is a virtue. (To keep the book brief, sources are given only for direct quotations.) Furthermore, there is every reason to believe that even this concise introduction to Lincoln will arouse in some readers the same fascination with him experienced by Americans in every generation since the Civil War. For such individuals, the bibliographical essay is provided.

In a professional career largely devoted to the study and teaching of Lincoln and his times, I have gone deeply in debt to many scholars, living and dead. I can thank them earnestly and admiringly, but I can never repay them. From my students and colleagues at San Diego State University I also learned much, for, I am happy to say, they were not easy to please. I am honored that Frank J. Williams, President of the Abraham Lincoln Association, read the whole manuscript—and also watched the videocassette—and made many suggestions for its improvement. He is one of the scholars to whom I am particularly indebted.

Others whose assistance, cooperation, and encouragement I gratefully acknowledge are John D. Criste, Nicole Sauviat Criste, Dina M. Lee, Martin Magaña, Mary C. Smalling, and, especially, my wife, Nell.

Ruth Cook of the Lincoln Museum, Fort Wayne, Indiana, Thomas F. Schwartz and Mary Michals of the Illinois State Historical Library, Springfield, and Lyn Olsson of Special Collections, San Diego State University, could not have been more generous in sharing their expertise and the resources of their institutions.

Above all, I wish to thank Gary L. Beebe, who introduced me to the educational potential of combining visual with written history. He not only conceived (and named) the "Out of the Wilderness" project—the production of a video documentary on Abraham Lincoln based upon a written biography of him—but inspired and supervised its completion. His belief that a video and book in combination would lead to a deeper and more personal understanding of Lincoln than either could by itself has, I think, been proved.

Prologue

In Springfield, Illinois, at 8:00 in the morning of February 11, 1861, Abraham Lincoln, president-elect of the United States, stood on the rear platform of the railroad car that would take him to Washington, D.C., for his inauguration. The conductor was about to pull the cord signaling the engineer to get underway when Lincoln began speaking to the estimated one thousand friends and fellow citizens who had gathered outside the Great Western depot to say good-bye.

"My friends," Lincoln began his extemporaneous remarks, "no one, not in my situation, can appreciate my feelings of sadness at this parting. To this place, and the kindness of these people, I owe everything. Here I have lived a quarter of a century.... Here my children have been born, and one is buried. I now leave, not knowing when, or whether ever, I may return, with a task before me greater than that which rested upon Washington.... Trusting in Him, who can go with me, and remain with you and be everywhere for good, let us confidently hope that all will yet be well. To His care commending you, as I hope in your prayers you will commend me, I bid you an affectionate farewell."

The conductor pulled the cord and slowly the train

chugged away from the station, the people waving and calling their own affectionate farewells.

It is safe to say that no president-elect leaving his hometown to become president of the United States was ever in so somber a mood. If his simple remarks were melancholy, even depressed, there was good reason for it, and the townspeople understood. Most of them may also have understood why he was uncertain he would ever see them again.

The nation of which Lincoln was soon to become the chief executive was in the process of disintegration, and he seemed destined to become the first president of a dis-United States. By the time he left Springfield, seven states of the Deep South had formally seceded from the Union, adopted a constitution for a new nation, the Confederate States of America, and elected as provisional president and vice-president two formidable Southern moderates, Jefferson Davis of Mississippi and Alexander H. Stephens of Georgia.

Without waiting for their new government to organize and begin its operations, the seceded states, one after the other, proceeded to seize U.S. forts, arsenals, and other federal property within their limits (except Fort Monroe, Virginia, Fort Sumter and Key West, South Carolina, and Fort Pickens in Florida), thus all but bringing an end to U.S. authority within the states of the Confederacy.

The mood of ardent Confederates was jubilant and optimistic, for, believing their new nation was founded on a principle to which all Americans were dedicated, they were confident of success. The Declaration of Independence of 1776—the first document to use the name United States of America—proclaimed that governments derived their just powers from the consent of the governed and that whenever any government exceeded its powers or became destructive of the ends for which it was established, it was, in the words of the Declaration, "the right of the people to alter or abolish it, and to institute new Government." This is the theory that justified the secession of the colonies from the British Empire, and millions of Americans in both North and South agreed that it equally justified the secession of states from the Union. As they saw it, the antislavery program of Lincoln and the Republican party exceeded the powers given to the central government by the Constitution and was destructive of the ends for which the union of states had been established. In seceding and forming a new government, supporters of secession believed that the Southern states were simply putting into practice a fundamental American political principle. In the event the new administration denied states the right of self-government (what in the next century would be called self-determination) and attempted to hold them in the Union by force, then the Confederates would fight Lincoln for their independence as their forebears had fought King George III for theirs.

Of course Lincoln and his Republican party had persuasive counterarguments and principles. They maintained that their policy of prohibiting slavery in the western territories while leaving it alone in the states was not a violation of powers, but was, in fact, authorized by article 4, section 3 of the Constitution, which gave Congress power to make rules and regulations for the territories. In their view, shared by many Democrats, there was, therefore, no justification for secession. Secession was nothing less than rebellion, and it would be the responsibility of the new president to suppress rebellion.

In efforts to prevent or delay the impending conflict (nobody even dreamed of the carnage the Civil War would bring), compromise proposals were submitted by Congress and by a convention of states meeting in Washington. But they were unacceptable to both Lincoln Republicans and Southern secessionists because compromise meant abandoning the principles to which they were ardently committed. Since neither side was willing to back down, a peaceful reunion early in 1861 was an impossibility. But the people of the time did not know that, and, in Lincoln's words, they could "confidently hope that all will yet be well." The hopes of the Unionists would have been more confident had some other Republican been elected president, for few people—including many residents of Springfield—believed that the uneducated and inexperienced Lincoln was capable of supplying the required leadership.

ONE

Lincoln's Youth

Lincoln was born in a one-room log cabin on the Sinking Springs farm near Hodgenville, Kentucky, on February 12, 1809. His parents, Nancy Hanks Lincoln and Thomas Lincoln, both born in Virginia, had been taken to Kentucky as young children and, experiencing the hardships and deprivations of life on the frontier, had grown up illiterate or, at best, semiliterate. It is possible that both parents could read a little, but Nancy could not write her name, and Thomas could write his, according to his famous son, only "bunglingly." Married in 1806 near Springfield, Kentucky, they lived for a time in Elizabethtown and in 1808 moved to the Sinking Springs farm, bringing with them their young daughter Sarah, born two years before the future president. Because of the ruggedness of the land and a deficiency in the title to the farm, the family moved ten miles east in 1811 to a farm on Knob Creek.

For many years no attention was paid to the cabin on the Sinking Springs farm in which Lincoln had been born, and in 1860 Lincoln himself, whose first memories were of Knob Creek, did not know exactly where the earlier farm had been located. In March 1861 a nearby farmer who did know purchased the remains of a cabin believed to have been the Lincoln birth cabin and moved it to his own farm. It remained

there until the mid-1890s, when Lincoln enthusiasts found
it and declared, more or less arbitrarily, that it was indeed
the cabin where Nancy Lincoln had given birth. It was then
moved back to the Sinking Springs farm, which a Lincoln
admirer had purchased. During the next few years it was
frequently dismantled, its logs carefully marked, and exhibited at fairs and expositions throughout the country. Upon
completion in 1911 of a memorial building on the spot
where it was thought the cabin had been located originally,
its travels came to an end. It was reassembled inside the
mausoleum and may be visited there today as the "traditional" birthplace cabin.

In December 1816, disputes over the exact boundaries
of the farm, and one feels sure, the restlessness of a pio-
neer dreaming of a better land and a better life "further
on," caused Thomas Lincoln to move his family again.
This time they moved ninety miles northward, crossed the
Ohio River, and settled near Little Pigeon Creek in the
midst of the thick forests of Spencer County in southern
Indiana. Lincoln later wrote that the move had been made
"partly because of slavery." If so, it was more likely a reflection of the difficulties experienced by poor white people in competing with the increasing number of black
slaves than of strong moral objections felt by Thomas toward slavery as an institution.

Though very young, Lincoln was large for his age and
an axe was put into his hands immediately. From that time
until he was twenty-three years old, he recalled, he was
scarcely ever without one except when he was plowing or
harvesting. So it must have seemed.

In 1818 an epidemic of "milk sickness"—a disease contracted by drinking the milk of cows that had eaten the

poisonous white snakeroot—afflicted southwest Indiana. Nancy Hanks Lincoln died of it in October at the age of thirty-five and was buried in a rough wooden coffin a quarter of a mile from the cabin. The year that followed was a wretched one for Thomas, his two young children, and one of Nancy's cousins, Dennis Hanks, who had come to live with the Lincolns in 1817. At eleven years of age, Sarah was unable to perform the chores of a grown woman, and though Dennis Hanks was nineteen, neither he nor Thomas was of much help as a homemaker. Finally, Thomas returned to Elizabethtown and in December 1819 married a recently widowed friend, Sarah Bush Johnston.

The new Mrs. Lincoln, thirty-two years old, had so many household goods—many of them true luxuries to the undersupplied Lincolns—that she had to transport them in a large wagon pulled by four horses. In addition to her pots, pans, blankets, and small furniture, she brought her own three children, Elizabeth, thirteen years old; John, ten; and Matilda, nine. Counting Dennis Hanks, that meant that eight people lived in the one-room cabin. Under the direction of the new lady of the house—often called "Sally," perhaps to avoid confusion with her stepdaughter, Sarah—physical improvements were soon made, a floor was laid, the loft in which Lincoln and John Johnston slept was probably enlarged, and with the addition of Sally's furniture, the primitive cabin became a comfortable, if crowded, home. The most important addition to the household, of course, was Sally herself. She put new clothes on Lincoln and Sarah so that as she put it, they "looked more human," fed them all well and kept them clean, and "proved a good and kind mother," as Lincoln later said.

Lincoln worked hard on his father's Indiana farm and while there, changed from a boy to a youth to an adult. Of his years in Indiana, Lincoln told a friend in 1859, "There was absolutely nothing to excite ambition for education." Yet something or someone had excited it in Lincoln. Perhaps it began earlier in one of the two schools near the Knob Creek farm he and Sarah attended for a few weeks. One specialist in Lincoln's youth says the boy could read and write at the age of seven. If true, it was an extraordinary achievement, suggesting not only that he was very bright but that the schoolmaster who lived across the road from the Knob Creek farm recognized it and gave him special tutoring. Perhaps Lincoln's ambitions for education was excited without being recognized in the "blab" or "ABC" schools Lincoln and Sarah attended in Indiana for about four months in 1822 and about six months in 1824. His stepmother, illiterate herself, recalled that Lincoln "was diligent for knowledge . . . and read all the books he could lay his hands on." "He read the Bible some," she continued, "though not as much as is said; he sought more congenial books suitable for his age." Foremost among these was *Aesop's Fables* and Weems's *Life of Washington*. When he came across a passage he liked, he would copy it with charcoal on a board if he had no paper. When he got some paper, he would recopy it and recite it out loud, then preserve it in a scrapbook.

On the Indiana farm Lincoln grew to be 6'4" tall and in his early twenties may have weighed over two hundred pounds. Because of his great size and strength, he was in much demand as a laborer in the growing settlements along Little Pigeon Creek. Accordingly, his father occasionally hired him out to split rails for fences, plow fields, butcher pigs, and perform other farming chores. One such experience, not involving farm work, must certainly have excited his ambition for education. A neighbor who owned a farm on the banks of the Ohio River hired Lincoln to operate a ferry across the Anderson River where it flowed into the Ohio near the town of Troy.

In his spare time Lincoln built himself a small, flat-bottomed scow and one day was asked by two travelers to take them and their baggage into the middle of the Ohio so they could catch a steamer. When his passengers climbed aboard the steamboat, each turned and tossed a silver half-dollar into Lincoln's scow. It was the first easy money Lincoln had ever made and it so impressed him that many years later, as president, he marveled over it to his secretary of state.

Even more stimulating in his awakening to the world beyond his father's farm was the flatboat trip he took down the Ohio and Mississippi rivers to New Orleans, 1,200 miles away. In cash-poor southern Indiana, settlers often paid for goods with the products of their farms, the merchants sometimes acquiring far more than they could consume. One such merchant was James Gentry, who owned a general store not far from the Lincolns. In 1828 Gentry hired Lincoln to help his son Allen build a flatboat for the sale of surplus pork, flour, meal, and other produce in Southern markets.

The flatboats in use on the western rivers at this time were usually about sixty-five feet long and eighteen feet wide, with four feet of freeboard in the center and a little house or cabin at the stern. The hull was built of poplar planks, bottom up, near the water's edge. When it was finished, one end of a rope was attached to the gunwale on one side and the other end thrown over the limb of a tree. Oxen then pulled the boat upright and it was rolled on logs into the water.

The two young men started to build their boat in October and were ready to depart in December, with Lincoln usually handling one of the forward sweeps or oars. Although they drifted with the current, it was not so easy as it sounds; they had to be constantly on the alert for sandbars, brush snags, and steamers inclined to show them little respect. At night they would sometimes tie up alongside other flatboats and exchange tall stories with their crews. The rivermen were a rough and heavy drinking lot who knew how to fight; they had to in order to survive. Their cargoes and the lumber in their boats were valuable, and they were subject to attack by gangs of outlaws or slaves. One night on the lower Mississippi Lincoln and Gentry were attacked by seven slave men who intended to kill and rob them. After a strenuous fight, they succeeded in driving the blacks off the boat, cut the line, and made for open water.

After selling their produce and their boat in New Orleans—the lumber from which was used in the building of houses and stores in the booming city—the two friends went sightseeing. The effect on Lincoln's mind of seeing so many vessels from ports all over the world tied up at the wharves, their masts and stacks forming a forest very different from any the young man had seen before; of the startling excitements and temptations of the renowned French Quarter; of the experience of personally observing the slave marts, where men, women, and children were merchandised like cattle must be left to the imagination, for Lincoln wrote and said little about it.

A representation of Lincoln as a flatboatman. (From *Frank Leslie's Illustrated Magazine*, courtesy of the Lincoln Museum, Fort Wayne, Indiana, a part of Lincoln National Corp.)

"If slavery is not wrong," Lincoln wrote a Kentucky editor in 1864, "nothing is wrong. I cannot remember when I did not so think, and feel." He had had contact with slavery all his life, but never before as it existed in New Orleans and the Deep South. He saw it exactly as we might view a morally reprehensible custom or institution in some foreign land—as something we were helpless to change but whose expansion into our own society we would strenuously resist.

The trip to New Orleans could not have failed to excite Lincoln's ambition and was probably a major factor in the estrangement with his father that came soon after his return to Indiana. Whatever caused the rupture between father and son, it was extreme and permanent. After the early 1830s they lived barely one hundred miles apart but seldom saw each other. Thomas Lincoln never met his daughter-in-law or any of his grandsons and never visited his son's home in Springfield.

Upon his return from New Orleans—he worked his way upriver on a steamboat—Lincoln began to attend court sessions held in the log courthouses of nearby Rockport and Boonville. He was fascinated by the arguments of the lawyers, and when he returned home would repeat them to anyone who would listen. The first law book he ever studied was a borrowed copy of *The Revised Laws of Indiana*, which included such documents as the Declaration of Independence and the Constitution of the United States as appendixes. He studied the book spellbound, though it was a few years yet before he realized he had found his professional career.

On his twenty-first birthday in February 1830, Lincoln was free of legal obligations to his father and could have struck out on his own, which he was eager to do. But he chose in March to help his family—now grown to thirteen members by the addition of Sally's sons-in-law and grand-children—move one last time to land on the north bank of the Sangamon River near Decatur, Illinois. The land had been chosen and partially cleared for them by John Hanks, another of Nancy Hanks Lincoln's cousins who had lived with the family off and on for several years. With Lincoln driving one of the three oxcarts loaded with fam-ily possessions, the 225-mile journey was completed in about two weeks.

Though the men quickly raised a log cabin—necessari-ly a large one this time—and planted a crop, some mem-bers of the family regretted the move. In the fall many of them were sick, and the winter of 1830–31—the winter of the Big Snow—was unusually severe. With thawing in the spring came serious flooding, and Thomas and Sally de-cided they had had enough and would return to Indiana. With several members of the family accompanying them, they got as far as some land near Charleston, Illinois, fifty miles away, where, worn out and discouraged, they stopped and stayed. Meanwhile, Lincoln, finally off on his own, was determined to make something of himself. He did not know what it would be, only that it would not involve full-time farming.

TWO

The New Salem Years

First, he went to work for one Denton Offutt, a promoter and speculator in central Illinois, now being settled, mostly by Southerners. Only a few years older than Lincoln, Offutt hired the newly independent young giant, his step-brother John Johnston, and John Hanks to build a flatboat on the Sangamon River a few miles west of the market town of Springfield. By mid-April 1831 the boat was finished and the four young men began another downriver journey to New Orleans with a cargo of pork barrels and corn. They had gone only a few miles down the Sangamon when they became stuck on a mill dam beneath the little village of New Salem.

Although Offutt was the head of the venture, it was Lincoln who provided the leadership in freeing the boat and whose size, strength, and good nature most impressed the villagers.

Lincoln and Offutt were also impressed with New Salem, and in July, after the successful completion of their trip, Offutt opened a store in the village close to the river and hired Lincoln as a clerk. Unlike farming, clerking in Offutt's store gave Lincoln time to read, participate in the local debating society, and, under the tutelage of the schoolmaster, Mentor Graham, study English grammar

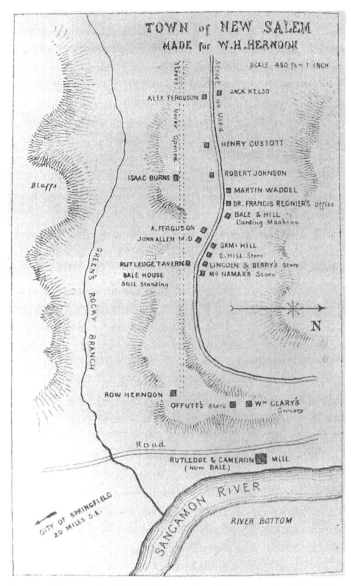

A map drawn for W. H. Herndon. (Courtesy of the Lincoln Museum, Fort Wayne, Indiana, a part of Lincoln National Corp.)

and mathematics. Few men on the farming frontier combined Lincoln's physical strength, ability to tell good stories, and ambition for education, and the newcomer soon
became one of the village's favorites. His popularity soon
led Jack Armstrong, leader of a rowdy group known as the
Clary's Grove Boys, to challenge him to a wrestling match.
There are several versions of the fight, but all agree that
it ended amicably and with lasting mutual respect. Although his ambition was elevating him above the society
in which he had grown up, Lincoln knew how to handle
western roughnecks.

The friendship and respect he had so quickly won in
New Salem buoyed Lincoln's confidence in himself, and
in March 1832, just six months after taking up residence
in the village, he announced himself as a candidate from
Sangamon County for the lower house of the state legislature in the capital, Vandalia. He issued a lengthy "Com-
munication" to the people of the county, written with the
help, it seems likely, of Mentor Graham. He favored government expenditure for railroads and for improving navigation upon rivers like the Sangamon and stated that education was the "most important subject which we as a
people can be engaged in." In short, he described himself
as a Henry Clay Whig who would use the power of government to improve the lives of the people.

At about the same time Lincoln announced the beginning of his political career, Offutt closed his store—leaving his clerk without income—and the governor of the
state called for volunteers against the Sac and Fox Indians
led by Chief Black Hawk. Lincoln enlisted in a militia
company and was quickly elected captain, thanks in part
to the backing of the Clary's Grove Boys; no success ever

gave him greater pleasure, he later stated. Lincoln saw no fighting in the fifty-one days he spent in the Black Hawk War, but remembered he had fought "a good many bloody struggles with the musquetoes [*sic*]."

After being discharged, Lincoln returned to New Salem only two weeks before the countywide election in August and had little opportunity to campaign. He lost, but was heartened because New Salem cast 277 votes for him and only 7 against, even though in the fall presidential elections it showed a distinct preference for Andrew Jackson over Henry Clay.

Reluctant to leave such good and generous friends, Lincoln looked about for a way to make a living in New Salem. At just the right moment, a merchant offered to sell his stock of goods to Lincoln and one William F. Berry on credit, and the two nearly impoverished men enthusiastically opened what they believed was *the* store in town. But Berry proved to be unreliable and a heavy drinker, and the store went deeper and deeper into debt. Finally, as Lincoln wrote, it "winked out." Berry died in 1835, leaving Lincoln with responsibility for $1,100 in debts, a huge amount.

In order to support himself and start retiring what he called the "national debt" (which he succeeded in doing in the 1840s), Lincoln acquired a compass and chain, read the appropriate how-to books, and became deputy surveyor of Sangamon County. He surveyed for roads in the rapidly growing area and platted several towns. In addition, he split rails, hired himself out to farmers, and took jobs as a handyman. Somehow he received the appointment as postmaster for New Salem, an office too insignificant for his politics to concern President Jackson, who signed his commission.

The office paid only fifty dollars a year plus free mailing privileges, but it was undemanding and gave Lincoln the opportunity to read all the newspapers subscribed to.

In 1834 he was elected to the state legislature, receiving the highest number of votes cast for any candidate. The office paid three dollars a day during the legislative session, which was usually about three months annually. While in Vandalia, Lincoln roomed with another legislator, John T. Stuart, an attorney in Springfield who encouraged him to study law and lent him the necessary books. Except when the legislature was in session, Lincoln applied himself to his studies with his customary diligence, and in the fall of 1836 was licensed to practice law in Illinois. He was reelected to the legislature the same year and again in 1838 and 1840.

As a resident of New Salem, Lincoln had no home of his own, though he could easily and quickly have built himself a cabin had he wanted to. He boarded around, often with Jack Armstrong and his wife, Hanna, who mended his clothes for him; with Mentor Graham; with Jack Kelso, who aroused his interest in literature by reading and reciting Shakespeare and Robert Burns at length; and with incidental travelers at the inn kept by James Rutledge. At night he most often slept in Offutt's store or his own or wherever he happened to be at bedtime.

At the Rutledge tavern Lincoln became well acquainted with the innkeeper's slender and beautiful nineteen-year-old daughter, Ann. It did not take him long to fall in love with her, but he could not declare himself because she was at the time betrothed to a man known as John McNeil, who had come to New Salem in 1829 and, unlike most other residents, managed to accumulate a significant amount of money. Suddenly, he told Ann that his real name was John MacNamar and that he must leave her temporarily to return to his home in New York and make provisions for his aging parents. He was gone a suspiciously long time and his occasional letters explaining the delay became increasingly formal. Then they ceased altogether and, like Ann herself, most of the townspeople believed he had no intention of returning and marrying her. She was now free to accept Lincoln's attentions.

By this time the Rutledges had moved a few miles to a farm purchased by MacNamar just before his departure, and Lincoln visited Ann there as frequently as he could, often spending the night at a nearby farm. The courtship lasted for several months, and in all probability the two lovers made plans for the future. Then Ann contracted a fever and died in August 1835. Lincoln took her death very hard, so hard that some of his friends feared he might take his own life.

The story of Lincoln's love for Ann Rutledge is based entirely upon reminiscences, the earliest being dated 1862, the rest after 1865, and some eminent historians have in the past dismissed it as a myth, a legend. But all of what is known about Lincoln's life in New Salem is based upon reminiscences and, as recent scholars have pointed out, there is no more reason to doubt Lincoln's romance with Ann Rutledge than there is to doubt his fight with Jack Armstrong.

THREE

Springfield and the Law

The eight years Lincoln spent in the Illinois state legislature would not have impressed most easterners. Six of the eight years were served in Vandalia, capital of Illinois from 1820 to 1839, a village of no more than eight hundred people and perhaps one hundred buildings, most of them made of logs. When Lincoln arrived for his first term in December 1834, the capitol was a two-story brick building that had been a bank and was rapidly deteriorating. The chambers occupied by both houses had been formed by knocking down walls and putting pillars in their place and were as unostentatiously furnished as a country inn. Members sat at long tables with cork inkstands before them. Beside them on the floor were wooden boxes full of sand for blotting ink on paper and for the accommodation of tobacco chewers. A fireplace and a stove provided heat, candles in tall holders light.

Conditions soon improved, but even a new and traditional state house built by the people of Vandalia in 1836 could not keep the capital from moving elsewhere. There was no arguing with a census in 1835 that showed the rapid growth of population northward, a growth reflected in a reapportionment of seats greatly increasing the influence of members from Sangamon County. A powerful bloc, they were successful in having an act passed in 1837 to move the capital to Springfield effective in 1839.

Springfield's population was only 1,500, but it was the center of a booming agricultural county of nearly 20,000 people. It had churches, schools, stores, taverns, doctors, lawyers, and a courthouse in which state business could be transacted. The Greek revival capitol, built on the town square, was not completed until 1853, though some parts of it were in use before then. The new capital was an improvement over the old, but most easterners would have considered Lincoln's eight-year experience in the Illinois legislature to be more nearly comparable to service in their county rather than their state governments.

It is hardly surprising that the contributions of the Illinois state legislature to Lincoln were greater than his contributions to it. The legislature increased his self-confidence by demonstrating to him that despite his lack of education and his isolation in the forests of Indiana during his formative years, he could hold his own with the political leaders of his adopted state, that, indeed, he *was* one of the political leaders of his state and of the Whig party in Illinois. In the legislature he came to know men who, in one way or another, would influence his own career: Edward D. Baker, Stephen A. Douglas, John J. Hardin, Lyman Trumbull, Orville H. Browning, and many others. He learned that the people can be wrong and that it is a leader's moral obligation to resist them when they are, not to yield to their wishes simply because he is their elected representative.

As a Whig, he strongly favored government subsidies for internal improvements, but he had known that the act passed in 1836 as a result of immense popular pressure

would be ruinous to the state's finances and in the end
would fail to attain its objectives. Yet he had voted for the
act, anyway. He also learned that there was no future for
him in New Salem (which ceased to exist in 1840) or even
in flourishing communities like Petersburg nearby. His
place, Lincoln now knew, was in a law office in the new
state capital.

When Lincoln rode into Springfield in April 1837 on a
borrowed horse, he carried a few dollars in cash and all of
his possessions—two or three law books and some clothing—in his two saddlebags. This after almost six years in
New Salem. Lincoln was a nonaccumulative man. If he had
had a cabin in New Salem, it would have been furnished
with Spartan simplicity; he cared nothing for ornamenta-
tion or personal adornment. Although he had purchased
a single bedstead upon his arrival, he learned upon inqui-
ry in the general store he had not enough money for a
mattress and blankets. He looked so forlorn that one of
the proprietors, Joshua Speed, a Kentuckian five years Lincoln's junior, offered to share his own room above the
store. Lincoln accepted and gratefully carried his saddlebags up the stairs. "Well, Speed," he said when he came
back down, "I'm moved."

For four years, until Speed moved back to Kentucky, Lincoln continued to room with Speed, who became his close
and intimate friend, perhaps the only one he ever had; for
in personal matters Lincoln was unusually reserved. The
personal matters about which Lincoln, twenty-eight years
old, and Speed, twenty-three, most often exchanged confi-
dences involved their relations with women.

In 1833, when he was still living in New Salem, Lincoln had met one Mary S. Owens of Kentucky, who was

ILLINOIS

INDIANA

New Salem •

⊙Springfield

Mississippi River

• Vandalia

Anderson River

Little Pigeon Creek

Troy

KENTUCKY

Ohio River

• Hodgenville

Lincoln Country

The state capitol, Springfield. (Courtesy of the Lincoln Museum, Fort Wayne, Indiana, a part of Lincoln National Corp.)

paying a brief visit to her sister. Three years later the sister told Lincoln she would bring Mary back to New Salem if Lincoln would marry her. Lincoln assented with some warmth; he remembered Mary as being attractive, intelligent, and agreeable. Mary returned to New Salem in November 1836 and remained until the spring of 1838. But Lincoln went to Vandalia to attend the legislature in December and moved to Springfield the following April, so they saw very little of each other.

What Lincoln did see did not please him, for Mary was now toothless and overweight and he suspected her of being much older than she claimed. In her letters to Lincoln, Mary indicated that she considered them to be truly engaged to be married, and, in his letters to her Lincoln equivocated, offering to release her from the obligation unless she was sure marriage to him would contribute to her lasting happiness. Mary could not fail to understand Lincoln's true feelings, and when, in the fall of 1837, as a matter of honor, Lincoln asked her to marry him, she surprised him by turning him down. It was a shock and at least a momentary humiliation, and Speed, who had been a party to the whole unhappy affair, tried successfully to show Lincoln how much better off both he and Mary were. Mary recognized it herself, recalling later that Lincoln had been "deficient in those little links which make up the chain of woman's happiness." To the wife of his friend Orville Browning, Lincoln wrote, "I most emphatically . . . made a fool of myself. I have now come to the conclusion never again to think of marrying; and for this reason; I can never be satisfied with anyone who would be block-head enough to have me."

Lincoln practiced law in Springfield with three different partners, all born in Kentucky, all Whigs in politics. First was John T. Stuart who, as a member of the state legislature, had convinced Lincoln that his lack of education would not prevent his becoming a lawyer. In a bitter campaign in 1838, Stuart defeated Stephen A. Douglas for one of the Illinois seats in the U.S. House of Representatives and was reelected two years later. The district he represented comprised nearly half the state, and Stuart spent much of his time keeping distant fences mended, leaving most of the law firm's business to its junior partner.

In 1841 Lincoln went into practice with Stephen T. Logan, the most respected member of the Sangamon County bar. Under Logan, Lincoln's legal education and proficiency were carried to a higher level than they had been under the often-absent Stuart. In fact, Logan thought that Lincoln did not know much law and impressed upon him the need for thorough research and the careful preparation of briefs and other legal papers. He did recognize Lincoln's knack of compelling witnesses to tell the truth even when they wanted to lie and his ability to "read" his juries.

In 1844 Lincoln, tired of the routine and clerical work that so often devolved upon him as a junior partner, started his own firm with William H. Herndon. Nine years younger than Lincoln, Herndon was working as a clerk in Joshua Speed's store in 1837 when Lincoln moved in and, like Lincoln, slept upstairs. He had attended Illinois College in Jacksonville for one year and in 1841, with Lincoln's encouragement and assistance, began to study law. The same year he was admitted to the bar, Lincoln took him on as a partner. Herndon admired Lincoln, whom he always addressed as "Mr. Lincoln," and though he was an

The Tinsley Building at Sixth and Adams, Springfield. Lincoln's law offices were on the third floor (*at left of photo*). (From *Frank Leslie's Illustrated Magazine*, courtesy of the Lincoln Museum, Fort Wayne, Indiana, a part of Lincoln National Corp.)

equal partner he assumed the role of subordinate. He managed the office, kept the books, and did much of the legal
research. Although he and Lincoln were unlike in many
ways, they got along well and their firm prospered. A major study now underway—"The Lincoln Legal Papers: A
Documentary History of the Law Practice of Abraham
Lincoln, 1836–1861"—shows that Lincoln was involved in
an astounding five thousand cases of all kinds, including
over three hundred appeals to the Illinois State Supreme
Court.

On the day before he left Springfield to become president, Lincoln paid his last visit to Herndon at their third-
story office on Fifth Street near the capitol. As he descend-
ed the stairs, he pointed to the "Lincoln and Herndon"
sign swinging on its rusty hinges at the bottom. "Let it
hang there undisturbed," he told Herndon. If he lived, he
would come back and they would go right on practicing
law "as if nothing had ever happened."

Springfield was the headquarters of the Illinois Eighth
Judicial District, comprising many of the counties in the
central and eastern parts of the state. For three months
every spring and three months every fall, the presiding
judge, accompanied by a retinue of attorneys, would make
the circuit of county seats to try whatever cases had aris-
en since their last visit.

Lincoln enjoyed these months riding the circuit, despite
the discomfort of travel by horse and buggy in all kinds
of weather and the primitive accommodations that were
often the only ones available at day's end. For reasons that
can only be surmised, he seldom returned to Springfield
on weekends, as the other attorneys did. He loved the fel-
lowship of the circuit and town after town, year after year,

William H. Herndon. (Courtesy of the Lincoln Museum, Fort Wayne, Indiana, a part of Lincoln National Corp.)

South side of state square, Springfield. The parade may have been part of an 1860 campaign rally or a victory celebration. (From *Frank Leslie's Illustrated Magazine*, courtesy of the Lincoln Museum, Fort Wayne, Indiana, a part of Lincoln National Corp.)

West side of state square, Springfield. (From *Frank Leslie's Illustrated Magazine*, courtesy of the Lincoln Museum, Fort Wayne, Indiana, a part of Lincoln National Corp.)

he made and renewed friendships. Clients flocked to him, and after court was adjourned for the day he was likely to find himself surrounded by townspeople eager to hear him talk about the issues of the time and to laugh at his jokes and funny stories. His repertoire of stories was endless and self-replenishing, and any incident would remind him of an anecdote. He had great powers of mimicry and appeared to "live" a story as he told it. Herndon recalled that Lincoln's "countenance and all his features seemed to take part in the performance. As he neared the pith or point of the joke or story every vestige of seriousness disappeared from his face. His little gray eyes sparkled; a smile seemed to gather up, curtain-like, the corners of his mouth; his frame quivered with suppressed excitement; and when the point or 'nub' of the story,—as he called it—came, no one's laugh was heartier than his."

Most of Lincoln's stories that have survived do not seem funny when read today. That is, of course, because it was the way he told them that was funny. "There was a zest and bouquet about his stories," wrote a young lawyer who often traveled the circuit with the future president, "that could not be translated or transcribed. One might as well attempt to reproduce the eloquence of Mr. Clay or the flaming anger of General Jackson. The story may be re-told literally, every word, period and comma. But the real humor perished with Lincoln."

When presenting an argument in court, delivering a political speech, or engaging in casual conversation with friends, Lincoln's face was expressive and alive. In repose it appeared to be sad, melancholy. "I never saw so gloomy and melancholy a face in my life," wrote Joshua Speed of Lincoln during the early Springfield years. Of Lincoln as president, the portrait painter Francis B. Carpenter declared he "had the saddest face I ever attempted to paint." Lincoln was a moody person without doubt, but he was no manic depressive, as some extremists have suggested. He was not even a true melancholic. Such individuals suffer abnormal inhibitions of mental and physical activity, and their condition becomes progressively worse. Lincoln was simply moody, and it is probable that frequently he was not nearly so dejected as he looked.

The city of Springfield grew rapidly once it became the state capital. Buildings filled up all the lots on the streets facing the square where the state house was being built—Washington and Adams on the north and south sides, Fifth and Sixth streets on the west and east—and on both sides of these streets as they approached the square. Offices, hotels, and taverns grew as if by magic on adjacent streets, and further out came comfortable houses and some residences almost large and elegant enough to be called mansions. In the 1840s and 1850s, Springfield was the social capital of Illinois as well as its political capital. When the legislature and state and federal courts were in session, it was a particularly lively place, with concerts, lectures, and theatrical performances to attend and, for the social and political elite, parties in the big houses.

FOUR

Marriage and Upward Mobility

Although Lincoln neither felt nor looked as if he belonged in Springfield's highest social circles, that is nevertheless where he found himself soon after his arrival. One of the most prominent leaders of Springfield society was Ninian Wirt Edwards, a merchant who had served briefly with Lincoln in the legislature. Edwards, whose father had been the last governor of Illinois Territory, a U.S. senator from Illinois, and governor of the state from 1826 to 1831, was married to Elizabeth Todd, a member of one of the leading families of Lexington, Kentucky. In 1839 a younger sister, Mary, came to Springfield to live in the Edwardses' home and in due course became acquainted with Lincoln, Stephen A. Douglas, and a surprising number of other eligible bachelors who went on to prominence in politics. Lincoln was uncomfortable around women, not good at drawing-room small talk, and unable to converse with the well-educated Mary about many of the subjects of interest to her. They were an oddly matched pair, Lincoln so tall and slim, Mary only 5'2" in height and plump in figure. But she recognized in Lincoln a quality and potential most others could not see, and he was attracted to her intelligence, warmth, and vivacity. Both were keenly interested in politics and avid readers of the newspapers. Sometime in 1840 they agreed to be married, though no formal announcement was made and he gave her no ring.

For reasons not definitely known but much speculated about, Lincoln broke off the engagement at the end of the year. It appears, as Lincoln's confidant Joshua Speed later wrote, that Lincoln was not "entirely satisfied that his heart was going with his hand." If so, Lincoln paid a high price for his romantic impulsiveness, experiencing—as he had after the death of Ann Rutledge—a prolonged period of extreme despondency. "I am now the most miserable man living," he wrote his partner John T. Stuart, then in Washington, on January 23, 1841. "If what I feel were equally distributed to the whole human family, there would not be one cheerful face on the earth. Whether I shall ever be better I can not tell; I awfully forebode I shall not. To remain as I am is impossible; I must die or be better."

Lincoln became better and could even have been happy, he wrote Speed a year later, except for the "never-absent idea, that there is one still unhappy whom I have contributed to make so. That still kills my soul." In the summer of 1842 he was still suffering moral torment. "I must regain my confidence in my own ability to keep my resolves," he told Speed. "In that ability, you know, I once prided myself as the only, or at least the chief, gem of my character; that gem I lost—how, and when, you too well know. I have not yet regained it."

Like Lincoln, Speed had long fretted over women, fearing he might not be cut out for marriage, fearing to make a lifelong commitment to his Kentucky sweetheart. But in February 1842 he did marry her. Eight months later Lincoln asked him an intimate question: "Are you now, in *feeling* as well as *judgement*, glad you are married?"

Speed's response was as prompt as it was positive, and within a month Lincoln and Mary Todd were married in the Edwardses' home. One thing was plain, Speed later wrote. "If I had not been married and happy—far more happy than I ever expected to be—he would not have married." No doubt Speed's happiness was a factor in Lincoln's seeking reconciliation and marriage with Mary, but so was Lincoln's need to regain the "chief gem" of his character, to become once again a man of his word.

The story that Lincoln broke his engagement and publicly humiliated Mary by simply failing to appear at their originally scheduled wedding ceremony is untrue.

The Lincolns moved into the Globe Tavern, a simple two-story wooden building, where they obtained board and room for four dollars a week. Several stage lines kept offices in the building and whenever a coach or a carriage pulled up in front a large bell on the roof would summon the stable hands to take care of the horses. It was a major step down for Mary, who was used to living in luxury, but she loved Lincoln and had confidence in his future. Soon after the birth of their first son, Robert Todd Lincoln, in August 1843, the couple rented a small cottage nearby. The next year, in May, they moved into a five-room bungalow (later enlarged) of their own on the northeast corner of Eighth and Jackson, for which Lincoln had paid $1,200 in cash plus a city lot. The house, the first and only one Lincoln ever owned, was located at the edge of town, but it was an easy six-block walk to the capitol. Here their second son was born in March 1846 and named Edward Baker Lincoln after one of Lincoln's good political friends.

The spring and fall months that Lincoln spent pleading cases in the county courthouses of the Eighth Judicial

Joshua Speed and Fanny Henning Speed. (Courtesy of the
Lincoln Museum, Fort Wayne, Indiana, a part of Lincoln
National Corp.)

Lincoln's Springfield home. (Courtesy of the Lincoln Museum, Fort Wayne, Indiana, a part of Lincoln National Corp.)

District, together with the profits earned by the firm of
Lincoln and Herndon, enabled him to pay off his "national
debt" and purchase his house. Traveling the circuit also
gave him the public exposure he needed as an ambitious
Whig politician, for politics and the law were his dual pro-
fessions. He was a natural politician, a man who could pack
them in around the stoves in small-town inns and stores
after court and, more often than not, turn strangers and
casual acquaintances into supporters. He did not have to
seek audiences; audiences sought him. The trouble was
that in Illinois there were more Democrats than Whigs in
the 1840s, and that meant intense competition between
Whig politicians for the few offices they could realistical-
ly hope to win.

Lincoln had two principal rivals for the Whig nomination for U.S. representative from the Seventh Congres-
sional District of Illinois: Edward D. Baker and John J.
Hardin, a cousin of Mary Lincoln. He lost some ground
to them because, not being a member of a church, he
lacked the denominational support they enjoyed. Another
factor that delayed his ambition to become a member of
Congress was that he, who twelve years before had arrived
on the Sangamon "a strange, friendless, uneducated, penniless boy, working on a flat boat—at ten dollars per
month," as he described himself, was being maliciously
represented as "the candidate of pride, wealth, and arris-
tocratic [*sic*] family distinction." It is no mystery which of
his opponents Lincoln held responsible for this political
demagoguery; he named his son after the other.

As it turned out, an agreement reached by the Whigs
of the Seventh District resulted in Hardin, Baker, and Lincoln being elected to serve consecutive single terms in

Congress. Lincoln's turn came in 1846, when he won an easy victory over the Democratic candidate. "Being elected to Congress," he wrote to Speed soon after the election, "has not pleased me as much as I expected." Perhaps he was displeased because, as the Constitution stood at the time, it would be thirteen months before he actually took his seat. Perhaps the election seemed an empty honor, since he knew that after his two-year term he would most likely have to make way for some other deserving Whig.

Lincoln had hoped that when the Thirtieth Congress finally convened in December 1847 the Whigs would have an opportunity to publicize (if not enact) their economic program for the nation. "The legitimate object of government," Lincoln believed—and the belief is what attracted him to politics and to the Whig party—"is to do for the people what needs to be done, but which they can not, by individual effort, do at all, or do so well, for themselves." He had in mind such things as building roads and bridges, improving rivers and harbors for navigation, establishing schools, and providing for "the helpless young and afflicted." But with a presidential election coming up in 1848, the Whigs were primarily interested in discrediting President James Knox Polk and the Democratic party for having "unnecessarily and unconstitutionally" begun the war with Mexico in 1846. Like a good Whig, Lincoln denounced Polk for insisting that Mexico had invaded the United States and that the war was therefore a defensive one, not a war for conquest. The president had abused his powers, Lincoln stated in a lengthy speech in January 1848, and was "a bewildered, confounded, and miserably perplexed man." As president, he would himself receive much similar—and more extreme—criticism.

Lincoln and the Whigs were no doubt sincere in their expressed revulsion against the Mexican War, but they were being purely pragmatic when they nominated one of the war's chief heroes, General Zachary Taylor, as their candidate for president in 1848. As Lincoln put it, he favored Taylor "because I am satisfied we can elect him, that he would give us a whig administration, and that we can not elect another whig." Taylor and his vice-presidential running mate, Millard Fillmore, a Henry Clay Whig, were duly elected, and on March 4, 1849, took their oaths of office. Lincoln's term in Congress had expired the day before.

Though out of office, Lincoln had good reason to expect he would have influence with the new Whig administration in the distribution of patronage. With mixed results he wrote many letters to President Taylor and members of his cabinet soliciting the appointment of friends in Illinois to various offices, and he worked very hard to have himself appointed commissioner of the General Land Office, a remunerative position in Washington just below cabinet rank. When he learned that a man in Chicago would likely receive the appointment, he asked the secretary of the navy (among others) to protest. At the time he and the secretary "were almost sweating blood to have General Taylor nominated," Lincoln declared that the man being considered for the land office had ridiculed the nomination of Taylor and supported Henry Clay. During the campaign this man had not even left Chicago, while Lincoln had made a speaking tour through New England for Taylor and spoken for him many times elsewhere. Though Lincoln's application was supported by the endorsements of influential members of the administration, many of these papers were apparently withheld from the president, and, much to Lincoln's resentment, the Chicagoan got the job.

Perhaps by way of compensation, Lincoln was offered the positions of both secretary and governor of Oregon Territory. Such jobs were often desired by out-of-office politicians, who could usually bring about their own elections to Congress when their territories were admitted to the Union as states. Much to Mary's relief, he declined both positions.

Disappointed with his brief foray into national politics, Lincoln concentrated his attention on his law practice, which grew and prospered as Illinois and the West grew and prospered. He gave speeches now and then, including a lukewarm eulogy on Zachary Taylor, who died in 1850, and a more ardent one on Henry Clay, who died in 1852. But between 1850 and 1854 there is very little political correspondence in the vast Robert Todd Lincoln Collection of his papers in the Library of Congress. Preoccupied with the law and his family—Eddie (four years old) died in February 1850; William Wallace Lincoln and Thomas (Tad) Lincoln were born in December 1850 and April 1853—he seemed destined to become the wealthy senior partner of a successful law firm. What political influence he exerted would be that of a power behind the scenes, not that of an officeholder.

Then, in 1854, his future changed and so did that of all Americans.

FIVE

The Spread of Slavery:
The Republican Victory in 1860

In an autobiographical sketch written for use in the 1860 presidential campaign, Lincoln said of himself: "In 1854, his profession had almost superseded the thought of politics in his mind, when the repeal of the Missouri Compromise aroused him as he had never been before."

What aroused Lincoln and many thousands of other Northerners was the passage by Congress in 1854 of the Kansas-Nebraska Act, which repealed the line drawn by the Missouri Compromise of 1820 across the western territory then owned by the United States. Under the terms of this compromise, slavery would be prohibited from the area north of the 36°30' line of latitude, or from the bulk of all the western lands. This confining of slavery was seen as a step toward the lessening of its influence in the country and, in some undefined way, as leading to the ultimate extinction of the institution. Repeal of the line, on the other hand, would permit the expansion of slavery into all the western territories, now greatly enlarged by the American acquisition after the Mexican War, and threaten to increase the influence and permanence of slavery. The author of the Kansas-Nebraska Act, which reversed United States policy on slavery, was the Lincolns' Democratic friend Senator Stephen A. Douglas.

He hated the repeal of the Missouri Compromise, Lincoln said in his first published speech attacking slavery on October 16, 1854. "I hate it because of the monstrous injustice of slavery itself. I hate it because it deprives our republican example of its just influence in the world; enables the enemies of the free institutions with plausibility to taunt us as hypocrites; causes the real friends of freedom to doubt our sincerity." The Constitution recognized and protected slavery and gave Congress no authority over it in the states. There could not have been a union of states, otherwise. But, Lincoln continued with emphasis, there was nothing in the Constitution that recognized or protected slavery in the territories. "I wish to make and to keep the distinction between the *existing* institution, and the *extension* of it so broad and so clear that no honest man can misunderstand me."

Lincoln was aroused by the repeal of the Missouri Compromise because he believed slavery was morally wrong and reflected grievously upon the republican experiment in government represented by the United States. His reemergence into politics, which became the dominant interest of his life, was the result of a moral passion and commitment unlike anything he had ever experienced before. Every one of the speeches he delivered between 1854 and his election to the presidency dealt with the urgency of preventing the expansion of slavery.

Public indignation against the Kansas-Nebraska Act among those Northerners who opposed slavery (not all Northerners did, by any means), was so strong that a new political party, the Republican party, was founded by antislavery Whigs and Democrats, and Lincoln soon became its leader in Illinois. He had been speaking and writing constantly against the repeal of the Missouri Compromise line, and in 1858 the Illinois Republicans nominated him to run for the U.S. Senate against Senator Douglas, who was seeking another term. The main feature of the campaign was a series of debates the two candidates engaged in before crowds of thousands in seven different Illinois towns. Douglas won reelection, but Lincoln had been so effective in stating the Republican arguments that overnight he became a national figure. Naturally there was talk about him as a possible presidential nominee in 1860. Was he presidential timber?

The Republicans of Illinois thought so and at a convention of the state party held in Decatur in May enthusiastically nominated him for president. When excitement was at its peak in the convention, John Hanks made a dramatic entrance into the hall carrying two fence rails with a placard attached to them: "ABRAHAM LINCOLN. The rail candidate for President in 1860. Two rails from a lot of 3,000 made in 1830 by John Hanks and Abe Lincoln." The delegates cheered and applauded. As soon as the noise subsided, Lincoln—"Honest Abe"—examined the rails with mock seriousness and then said he could not be sure he had split these exact same rails, but he had split a great many better ones in his time.

Enthusiastic for the "Rail Splitter" candidate as they were, most Illinois Republicans did not really believe he would be able to win the nomination away from William H. Seward of New York at the national nominating convention in Chicago. A graduate of Union College, Seward was a former governor of New York and since 1848 one of his state's U.S. senators. But in his long and active career, Seward had made political enemies and might not run well in some key states.

As a new political personality, a freshness and excitement attached to Lincoln. Having been born in a slave state was advantageous, too. For the Republican party was much criticized for being purely Northern. The fact that he had been born in a log cabin, grown up in the western wilderness, and split rails attracted him to old-line Whigs who had to play down their middle-class, business-oriented popular image. Yet as a former Whig himself, Lincoln was safe on such questions as the tariff and internal improvements. In short, Lincoln was a supremely "available" candidate and beat Seward for the nomination on the third ballot. Hannibal Hamlin of Maine, a former Democrat, was nominated for vice-president to balance the ticket.

The Democratic party split in two in 1860, thus assuring Lincoln's election. Stephen A. Douglas was the nominee of the traditional party and John C. Breckinridge of Kentucky, the vice-president of the United States, was nominated by Southern Democrats unwilling to accept Douglas. Because Lincoln, Douglas, and Breckinridge all stood for policies that were bound to create turmoil within the country, a fourth party, the Constitutional Union party, standing vaguely for the Constitution and the Union, was formed with John Bell of Tennessee as its nominee.

Although Lincoln and the Republicans received only 39.8 percent of the popular vote in the election, they received a substantial majority in the electoral college. Lincoln carried all the free states except New Jersey, whose electoral votes he split with Douglas. Besides the electoral votes from New Jersey, Douglas received only those of

Missouri. Although he was second in the number of popular votes, he was last in electoral votes. Breckinridge carried all the slave states except Kentucky, Tennessee, and Virginia, which went to Bell. But Breckinridge won the popular vote in only five Southern states. In fact, 55 percent of the Southern popular votes were cast for Douglas or Bell, both strong Unionists, a fact that made Republican strategists believe that even if secessionists should win control of their state governments they would not be able to hold it for long.

Lincoln's election caused secessionist fever to sweep across the Deep South and led to the formation of the Confederate States. With the nation trembling on the brink of dissolution or war, many Northerners, including some Republicans, urged the president-elect to reassure the South that he had no intention of interfering with slavery within the Southern states. "I have said this so often already," he replied to one correspondent, "that a repetition of it is but mockery, bearing an appearance of weakness, and cowardice, which perhaps should be avoided." Others beseeched Lincoln to make some compromise that would restore national unity. To one man who pleaded for compromise Lincoln said, "We have just carried an election on principles fairly stated to the people. Now we are told in advance the Government shall be broken up unless we surrender to those we have beaten." "By no act or complicity of mine," he told a New Englander, "shall the Republican party become a mere sucked egg, all shell and no principle in it."

SIX

An Underestimated Westerner

While waiting in Springfield for the time to leave for Washington, Lincoln issued no public reassurance of his essential moderation on the slavery issue and steadfastly refused to make any compromise on his stand against the spread of slavery. Because he was largely unknown outside his own state, the people of other states wondered about the character and capacity of the man to whom they had entrusted their fate and the fate of the nation. In the age before mass-reproduced photographs, the people were dependent upon drawings and prints and the reports of newspaper correspondents for portraiture. Since Lincoln had had so little opportunity to demonstrate his abilities of leadership, most of the reports focused on his appearance for clues to his character. Many of them were not at all flattering.

By 1860 Lincoln was no longer the robust young giant of his rail-splitting and flatboatman days. Now he was tall and thin, his weight dropping to 180 pounds, and though he retained much of the strength of his youth in his arms (and delighted in demonstrating it, as he also enjoyed comparing heights with other tall men), his spareness and stooped posture gave him the look of a consumptive.

But it was his face more than his cadaverous figure that

Lincoln the rough-hewn westerner. (Courtesy of the Lincoln Museum, Fort Wayne, Indiana, a part of Lincoln National Corp.)

Lincoln the rough-hewn westerner. (Courtesy of the Lincoln Museum, Fort Wayne, Indiana, a part of Lincoln National Corp.)

most often caused adverse reactions. Lincoln's face is so familiar to us (at least in its most flattering poses) that we have to make a special effort to see it as it appeared to people who were not familiar with it—observe his long, scrawny neck, his deep facial lines, his sunken cheeks, his large nose and enormous ears, his dark and often unkempt hair. To many of his contemporaries he looked like a yokel, a hayseed, a country bumpkin. "We must accept the results of universal suffrage," wrote the New England philosopher Ralph Waldo Emerson after the election, "and not try to make it appear we can elect fine gentlemen . . . [who would] please the English or French." When William H. Russell, the American correspondent of the *London Times*, pointed out Lincoln to an English friend toward the end of 1861, the friend exclaimed, "I give up the United States."

By the time of his election, the West of Lincoln's boyhood and youth had become a booming agricultural region, its prosperous cities and towns linked by railroads and boasting an abundance of churches, schools, and business for lawyers. Lincoln himself had experienced a material and intellectual development along with his section, but it did not register on him personally. His appearance recalled the old West, not the new, the wilderness West of dense forests, log cabins, and travel by ox cart. Wherever he went, Lincoln carried the frontier with him.

Although Lincoln always regretted his lack of education, he was probably not self-conscious about how he looked until the middle 1850s when his practice as a lawyer brought him into contact with big-city attorneys with more formal training and more conventional looks. Within days after being elected president, he began to grow a beard.

It is true that facial hair, most recently encountered by Americans during the Mexican war, was becoming stylish in the 1840s and 1850s, but as president Lincoln helped to set the style. His predecessor in the White House was clean shaven, as was his successor, and so were many other political leaders of the Civil War. Most likely Lincoln felt that a beard would fill in the hollows and soften the lines of his face, making him look more dignified, more presidential. Possibly he was influenced—certainly he was amused—by a letter sent before the election by a girl in New York State. He would be better looking with a beard, eleven-year-old Grace Bedell told him, and would win more votes. Grace was among those at the railroad station at Westfield, New York, when Lincoln's train stopped there en route to Washington. The president-elect asked for her, thanked her for her suggestion, and, to the delight of the crowd, lifted her up and kissed her.

In the nineteenth century it was not the custom for presidential candidates to travel about the country giving speeches and asking for votes. Between his nomination by the Republican party in May and his election in November 1860, Lincoln never left Springfield, though he attended hometown rallies and carried on an extensive correspondence with influential Republican leaders and newspaper editors, many of whom traveled to Illinois to confer with him. The voters, at least the readers among them, were well acquainted with Lincoln's views and those of the Republican party on the divisive issue of the time, the expansion of slavery, but they were not acquainted with Lincoln himself, a newcomer on the national political scene. That is why his train took a circuitous route and twelve days to get to Washington. At small towns all along the way, the train stopped for fuel and water and he appeared and spoke briefly to enthusiastic crowds. "I have come to see you and allow you to see me," he told the people at Little Falls, New York, "and in this so far [as] regards the Ladies, I have the best of the bargain on my side. I don't make that acknowledgement to the gentlemen." He deliberately avoided controversy at these stops, but did not rein in his good humor.

At major cities Lincoln spoke at greater length, expressing his faith that, for the sake of their children and all posterity, the American people would support his administration in its efforts to maintain the government. If states could secede at will, he told a large throng gathered beneath the balcony of his hotel in Indianapolis, Indiana, then the Union "would not be anything like a regular marriage at all, but only . . . a sort of free-love arrangement."

Addressing the state senate of New Jersey at Trenton, he spoke of having read Weems's *Life of Washington* when a boy and of having been especially impressed by the account of Washington's crossing of the Delaware River at Trenton. "I recollect thinking then, boy even though I was," he said, "that there must have been something more than common that those men struggled for." It was something more than independence from England; it was a promise of liberty "to all the people of the world to all time to come." At Independence Hall in Philadelphia, Pennsylvania, where the Declaration of Independence had been adopted, he again speculated about the meaning of the Revolution. The famous Declaration had been about more than the separation of the colonies from England. It had been about "giving liberty, not alone to the people of this country, but hope to the world for all future time." The

Declaration had given promise "that in due time the weights should be lifted from the shoulders of all men, and that *all* should have an equal chance." Could the country be saved on the basis of that promise? he asked. "If it can, I will consider myself one of the happiest men in the world if I can help to save it. . . . But, if this country cannot be saved without giving up that principle—I was about to say I would rather be assassinated on this spot than surrender it."

SEVEN

Disunion and the Outbreak of War

The long, jolting, stopping, and starting journey to Washington was a triumphant success, and Lincoln's spirits rose as a result of the unexpected magnitude of support demonstrated by people in the North. At the same time, incidents along the road and the threatening letters he had received at Springfield increased his awareness that he had bitter and extreme enemies who read the Declaration of Independence differently than he did. Secessionists and their many supporters in the North stood on the self-determination principle of the Declaration, which would allow the states to order their internal institutions as they chose. Lincoln and the Republicans did not disagree with this principle, but they were also attracted to the Declaration's principle of ultimate equality for all, a principle that represented a clear, though distant, threat to Southern civilization.

After the election in November 1860, scarcely a day passed when Lincoln did not receive threats that he would never live to take the presidential oath of office on March 4, 1861, along with about as many friendly letters urging him to be on the alert for plots against him. Beginning in Indiana, where an obstruction was found on the tracks capable of causing a derailment, a pilot engine preceded his train. In Ohio a newspaper reported that a bomb had been discovered in a carpetbag in his car. In Philadelphia, the night before speaking at Independence Hall on what the Declaration of Independence meant to him, Lincoln learned from two separate and reliable sources of a conspiracy to assassinate him as he passed through the ardently prosecessionist city of Baltimore, Maryland. At the insistence of General Winfield Scott, ranking officer in the U.S. Army, and Senator Seward, soon to become secretary of state, he quietly changed his plans, passed through Baltimore in the middle of the night on a special train, and arrived safely at his suite in Willard's Hotel, Washington, early in the morning of February 23. His wife, Mary, and their three sons joined him later in the day.

The trip was over, but Lincoln's secret arrival in Washington was ridiculed in the Democratic press. There had been no "Baltimore plot" against him, the opposition insisted, and columnists and cartoonists competed with each other in portraying the president-elect as a fool and a coward. According to his friend and self-appointed bodyguard Ward Hill Lamon, Lincoln always regretted having "sneaked" into the capital and thereafter refused to be intimidated by the continuing threats against his life.

While awaiting his inauguration, Lincoln attended a reception in his honor in Congress, called upon members of the U.S. Supreme Court, and conferred privately and at length with the men he had chosen to join his cabinet and with large numbers of individuals seeking jobs or hoping to influence the policy of his administration. Not all of the latter treated him with respect, considering him ill-informed and unsuited to the office he was about to assume. To one such group who had conferred with him in his hotel, he said as he escorted them to the door, "Well, gentlemen, I have been wondering, if Mr.Douglas or Mr. Bell had been elected President, you would have dared to talk to him as freely as you have to me."

On March 4 Lincoln and retiring president James Buchanan rode up Pennsylvania Avenue to the Capitol in an open carriage. Armed soldiers, together with specially recruited volunteers, lined both sides of the street, sharp-shooters were placed on rooftops to watch the windows opposite them, and artillery was moved into places where the crowd was thickest at the Capitol's east front. At about 1:00 on a bright and clear afternoon, Lincoln stood before a small table on the portico and read his Inaugural Address.

In this conciliatory speech Lincoln reassured the Southern states that he had no authority and no inclination to interfere with slavery within their limits and declared that the Union was older than the states and that no state could lawfully withdraw from it. Revolution would be justified, he conceded, if the majority deprived a minority of any clearly written constitutional right, but no such rights had been violated in the present case. The central idea of secession was anarchy, Lincoln said. "In *your* hands, my dissatisfied fellow countrymen," he concluded, "and not in *mine*, is the momentous issue of civil war. The government will not assail *you*. You can have no conflict without being yourselves the aggressors. *You* have no oath registered in Heaven to destroy the government, while *I* shall have the most solemn one to 'preserve, protect, and defend' it."

The Civil War began five weeks later, early on the morning of April 12, 1861, when Confederate batteries in Charleston, South Carolina, opened fire on Fort Sumter, which dominated Charleston harbor. The fort surrendered formally on April 14. Lincoln's response was prompt. The next day he issued a proclamation stating that the Constitution and laws of the United States were being resisted in seven states "by combinations too powerful to be suppressed" by the ordinary procedures. He therefore called for the states to supply a total of 75,000 soldiers to suppress the illegal combinations. At the end of the month, Jefferson Davis sent a message to the Confederate Congress in Montgomery referring to Lincoln's proclamation as a "declaration of war against this Confederacy." That's what it was, all right; now the question became, how would the country, North and South, respond?

It did not take long to find out. Virginia seceded on April 17, except for its western counties that refused to go along and soon became the state of West Virginia. Arkansas seceded on May 6, Tennessee on May 7, and North Carolina on May 20. Unionists, who had remained in control of these states after Lincoln's election, lost out to secessionists after the April 15 proclamation. In the slave states of Maryland, Kentucky, and Missouri, timely and aggressive action by Lincoln prevented secession, but most of their people remained sympathetic to the South and hostile to Lincoln and his war. Governments-in-exile were organized in Kentucky and Missouri and were represented by stars in the Confederate flag.

In the North the firing on Fort Sumter had a Pearl Harbor impact upon public opinion, uniting it, if only briefly, behind the Lincoln administration. The Confederates had fired on the flag; that made them rebels and traitors.

Looking back to this time in his Second Inaugural Address, March 4, 1865, Lincoln observed that "both parties deprecated war; but one of them would *make* war rather than let the nation survive; and the other would *accept* war rather than let it perish. And the war came." That is how it looked to Unionists, but as Jefferson Davis and the Confederates saw it, it was the North that made war and the South that accepted it.

EIGHT

The North as Underdog

The South accepted war in 1861 with enthusiasm and confidence; it had very good reasons to think it would win. Its disadvantages in troop numbers, industrial plants, railroads, and financial institutions have been so often stressed that they are obvious to us and seem to make victory for the North inevitable. What we do not understand is that the South's disadvantages were equally obvious to Southern leaders at the time, and *still* they and their followers thought their prospects were very bright. Otherwise they never would have led their people into war. Contrary to the conventional assumption, the North, not the South, was the underdog in the Civil War. The South's population was much smaller than the North's, yes, but it did not need so many soldiers to fight the defensive war it planned. A military rule of thumb was that the offensive side must have a three-to-one superiority over the defensive side, a ratio the North could not expect to meet. Fighting on its interior lines, Southern military leaders believed they could prevent the North from assembling more than a two-to-one superiority at any given point and time. Furthermore, the South was a vast region, about equal in size to the North minus the Pacific Coast states, which were too far away to figure in the fighting. How could the North subdue such a vast region? The South did not have to conquer the North; all it had to do was keep on fighting until the heavy casualties always suffered by the offensive side would sicken the people of the North and force the government to make a peace recognizing the independence of the Confederacy. After the war, Confederate general Pierre T. Beauregard declared that "no people ever warred for independence with more relative advantages than the Confederates."

One reason Americans think of the South as the underdog in the Civil War instead of the North is that they imagine the U.S. government in the early 1860s to have been the powerful political agency that it became as a result of the war and that it is now. The truth is very different. Early national leaders like George Washington, Alexander Hamilton, and John Marshall had believed in a strong central government, but in 1861 the government was so weak, the Union Lincoln inherited so loose, that eleven states tried to shake themselves out of it, and many Northerners wondered why on earth they should not be allowed to.

In his Farewell Address to the American people in 1796, George Washington stressed the necessity of maintaining a strong central government to keep the union of states together. In his 1837 Farewell Address President Andrew Jackson expressed a contrary view. He advised every friend of free institutions "to maintain unimpaired and in full vigor the rights and sovereignty of the States and to confine the action of the General Government strictly to the sphere of its appropriate duties." In the generation before the Civil War, the American people had heeded Jackson's advice, not Washington's. The result was that the only agency capable of maintaining the Union was weak, seemingly far too weak to do what was required of it.

The political development of the United States, in other words, had lagged far behind its economic and industrial development. "We have never been a nation," wrote the New York diarist George Templeton Strong as late as August 1864, "we are only an aggregate of communities, ready to fall apart at the first serious shock and without a center of vigorous national life to keep us together. . . . The bird of our country is a debilitated chicken, disguised in eagle feathers."

Even if somehow the North succeeded in subduing the South, would it be the same as preserving the Union? In his 1860 annual message to Congress President Buchanan had said, "The fact is that our Union rests upon public opinion and can never be cemented by the blood of its citizens. . . . If it cannot live in the affections of the people, it must . . . die." A Union in which states were held together by military force would be a despotism. Yet Lincoln was determined to use all the force necessary to preserve the Union. With the odds against him, he was gambling for fabulously high stakes. For the real issue of the war Lincoln was willing to fight to defeat secession involved much more than the preservation of the United States. It involved the survival of the whole idea of free republican government. The struggle with the South, he told Congress in a special message on July 4, 1861, "presents to the whole family of man the question whether a constitutional republic or democracy—a government of the people by the same people—can, or cannot, maintain its territorial integrity, against its own domestic foes. It presents the question, whether discontented individuals, too few in numbers to control . . . according to organic law . . . can . . . break up their Government, and thus practically put an end to free government upon the earth."

NINE

War and Disaster in the East

If Lincoln believed on April 15 that 75,000 soldiers would be enough to break up the disloyal combinations in the South and repossess the forts and other United States property they had seized, he learned better very quickly; by July 1 nearly 187,000 men were under arms. In the middle of the month some 35,000 of them under the command of General Irwin McDowell crossed the Potomac on a campaign to end the rebellion by capturing the Confederacy's new capital at Richmond, Virginia, one hundred miles away. The public, if not the venerable general-in-chief, Winfield Scott (whose career dated back to the War of 1812), was confident of success and confident that success would end the rebellion.

But on July 21, only twenty miles from Washington—at Bull Run, Virginia (or, as the Southerners called it, Manassas)—the Union army was repulsed by Confederate forces, and its untrained volunteers fled in panic back to Washington. It was a humiliating defeat, but it taught Northern Unionists that they faced a real war, not just a police action, and that they would have to mobilize their troops and resources on a scale not before imagined. Congress promptly authorized the enlistment of a million volunteers to serve for three years. By war's end, some two million men had served the Union, about three-quarters of a million the Confederacy.

A few days after the defeat at Bull Run, the field command of all U.S. troops was given to thirty-five-year-old George B. McClellan, a West Point graduate and Mexican War veteran. McClellan was a superior army administrator and drillmaster and soon turned his soldiers into a well-disciplined and well-equipped army, the Army of the Potomac. But months passed and he did nothing with it, perhaps in part because, having allowed himself to be hailed as the "young Napoleon" who would end the war in a single, professionally conducted campaign against Richmond, he was plagued by self-doubt. He was contemptuous of Lincoln, whom he considered his social and intellectual inferior, and was rude to him on several occasions. Lincoln said that he would hold McClellan's horse for him if only he would bring success.

Finally, McClellan transported his huge army down Chesapeake Bay to the tip of the peninsula formed by the York and James rivers and marched on Richmond from the southeast. The three-month campaign, featuring bloody battles as the Confederates resisted McClellan's advance up the peninsula, ended in early July after the Seven Days' battle, with the spires of the Rebel capital in the background. McClellan, a Democrat who had supported Stephen A. Douglas for president, blamed his failure on his Republican enemies in Congress, upon Secretary of War Edwin M. Stanton, and upon his commander-in-chief.

On July 8, Lincoln visited him at his supply base at Harrison's Landing on the James. McClellan handed the president a self-serving letter in which he insulted him by telling him that the rebellion had assumed the character of war. The war should be fought, he said, according to the highest Christian principles, with no unnecessary interference with Southern civilians or their property, including, emphatically, their slave property. Any radical action against slavery would cause the U.S. armies to disintegrate.

Lincoln read the letter in McClellan's presence. But because it was so easy to see that the general, having failed to achieve the long-promised military victory, was preparing himself for action in the field of politics, he said nothing.

The principal command of U.S. forces in the eastern theater of operations now shifted to General John Pope and the recently organized Army of Virginia. Pope, whose victories in the West had brought the upper half of the Mississippi under Union control, had known Lincoln in Illinois and conferred with him recently in Washington. Upon assuming command, he issued orders making it clear—with Lincoln's obvious approval—that, unlike McClellan, he would be no scrupulous observer of the liberty and property of disloyal civilians. He meant to wage in 1862 the kind of warfare successfully practiced in 1864 and 1865 by Generals Ulysses S. Grant and William Tecumseh Sherman, and might have done so except that at the end of August he was defeated at the battle of Second Bull Run and relieved of his command. This time, however, the defeated army retreated to Washington in good order.

Pope's defeat, following so soon after McClellan's, caused a fog of gloom to settle across the North. Increased dissatisfaction with the Lincoln administration was expressed in the press and among members of Lincoln's own Republican party. The feeling against the president among many Democrats was already so intense that he could not afford to alienate many more of them and hope to continue the war. That is one reason why, against the advice of most of his cabinet, Lincoln now restored McClellan to the chief command in the East. Democrats may have been appeased, but many Republicans were outraged.

At Antietam, Maryland, on September 17, McClellan stopped Confederate General Robert E. Lee, who was undertaking his first invasion of the North. The victory in this bloodiest single day in the Civil War—indeed, in American military history—gave Lincoln the opportunity to issue a proclamation he had been holding impatiently for several weeks.

Though Lee retired from the battlefield, he did not re-treat back into Virginia, and Lincoln urged McClellan not to let him do so. "If we cannot beat the enemy where he now is," the president exclaimed in frustration, "we never can." Early in October he paid a visit to the headquarters of the Army of the Potomac, but nothing he said could induce McClellan to move. Lee crossed the river, and when McClellan finally followed him, it was too late. That was the end of McClellan's military career.

Next in the unhappy sequence of Union commanders of the Army of the Potomac was Ambrose Burnside, who did not want the command and said he was unfit for it. The battle of Fredericksburg in December 1862 proved that he was right. Lincoln, the army, and the Unionists of the North were sickened and in despair.

After Burnside, Joseph Hooker, "Fighting Joe," was giv-en command of the Army of the Potomac. He succeeded in raising the morale of his troops—perhaps because he allowed prostitutes, "hookers," the freedom of the army's camps—but he was confused and badly beaten at Chan-cellorsville in May 1863. The public was appalled; the ad-

ministration was spending the blood and lives of its soldiers on a frightful scale and accomplishing nothing. When
Lincoln learned that Hooker had been defeated, he burst
out to a visitor in the White House, "If hell is . . . worse
than this place has been for the last year, I can't help sym-
pathizing with the Devil."

On June 28, Hooker yielded command to General
George Meade, the fifth commander of the Army of the
Potomac in ten months. Meade was a competent general
and stopped Lee's second invasion of the North in three
days of fierce fighting at Gettysburg, Pennsylvania, July 1,
2, and 3.

Casualties on both sides were very high, but at least the
Union had scored a victory. In an order congratulating his
troops, Meade declared he looked "to the Army for greater
efforts to drive from our soil every vestige of the presence
of the invader." When Lincoln read this order, he cried
out in anguish, "Drive the invaders from our soil! My God!
is that all?" Turning to John Hay, one of his private secretaries, he said, "This is a dreadful reminiscence of Mc-
Clellan. . . . Will our generals never get that idea out of
their heads? *The whole country is our soil!*"

Like McClellan after Antietam, Meade allowed Lee's
defeated army to get away. Lee was trapped north of the
flooded Potomac River and could not escape. But Meade
allowed him to wait until the river had subsided and then
build pontoon bridges across it. Lee did not escape; he
simply walked away. Again Hay recorded Lincoln's distress.
"We had them within our grasp," said the president. "We
had only to stretch forth our hands and they were ours.
And nothing I could say or do could make the Army move.
. . . If I had gone up there, I could have whipped them

myself." "What does it mean, Mr. Welles?" he asked the secretary of the navy. "Great God, what does it mean?"

It meant that after seven major battles and almost as many defeats, Lincoln had still not found a commander for the eastern theater who understood that Union victory required the destruction of the South's armies, not simply their defeat, and the crushing of Southern ability and will to raise new armies.

TEN

War and Progress in the West: Ulysses S. Grant

There *was* such a man in the western theater: Ulysses S. Grant. Like most others in April 1861, Grant assumed that the war against the South would be a limited one, that as soon as the Union won a major battle the Confederacy would collapse. In February 1862, while McClellan was still only drilling the Army of the Potomac, Grant did win a major battle, capturing Forts Donelson and Henry in Tennessee and taking 22,000 prisoners. This victory compelled the Confederacy to withdraw its troops from Kentucky and Missouri and a large part of Tennessee. But the Confederacy did not collapse. Instead in April, it counterattacked in force and almost defeated Grant at Shiloh, in southern Tennessee. After Shiloh, Grant later wrote, "I gave up all idea of saving the Union except by complete conquest of the South."

As McClellan had stated to Lincoln in his Harrison's Landing letter of July 1862, the principles of limited war provided that a Union army invading the South would confine its operations to fights against Southern armies, avoiding the destruction of private property, whether of civilians loyal to the United States or to the Confederate

States. After Shiloh, Grant recognized that this was the road to prolonged military stalemate, not victory for the United States. He therefore adopted a new policy that would, finally, bring an end to the war. Grant treated *all* civilian property that could be used to supply or sustain a Southern army exactly as if it were conventional contraband of war like arms and munitions. The destruction of such supplies could be accomplished without taking the lives of civilians and, in its effect, was the same as destroying enemy armies. Lincoln also recognized the necessity of expanding the war beyond the rules of traditional limited wars, and in September 1862 went beyond anything Grant or Pope had been authorized to do in the confiscation of the property of Southerners.

In 1863 Grant moved his army down the Mississippi to the Confederate fortress at Vicksburg and, after a brilliantly conducted siege, captured the city on July 4, the same day as Lee's retreat from Gettysburg.

In March 1864 Lincoln brought Grant to Washington, gave him command of all the U.S. armies, and told him to go out and win the war. "The particulars of your plans," he told Grant, "I neither know or seek to know."

At last Lincoln had found a general who knew what had to be done to win the war and whom he could trust to go out and do it.

ELEVEN

Life in the White House

Only one child, the ten-year-old son of President John Tyler twenty years earlier, had lived in the White House—or Executive Mansion as it was known officially—before the Lincolns moved in with their three sons in March 1861. Robert, now seventeen and a student at Harvard, was away most of the time, but for Willie age ten, and Tad seven, the old house was the site of endless adventures. They explored every room from the basement to the roof and enjoyed dashing noisily about on the first floor, which during the day was crowded with military and civilian officials and visitors of all kinds. Tad was known to have pulled a few unsuspecting beards. The boys had ponies of their own in the stables, and their two goats were said to have been escorted at least once to the second-floor living quarters.

In Springfield Lincoln had spent a good deal of time—much of it abstracted—with his young sons, but he saw much less of them, and of Mary, in Washington. Always a light sleeper, military and political problems often kept him awake far into the night, and he was usually in his second floor office by 7:00 A.M. Believing that the leader of a republic should be accessible to the people, he often set aside two or three hours on weekdays for people to come to him with their problems and requests, referring to these ses-

Robert Todd Lincoln. (Courtesy of the Lincoln Museum,
Fort Wayne, Indiana, a part of Lincoln National Corp.)

William Wallace "Willie" Lincoln. (Courtesy of the Lincoln Museum, Fort Wayne, Indiana, a part of Lincoln National Corp.)

Thomas "Tad" Lincoln. (Courtesy of the Lincoln Museum, Fort Wayne, Indiana, a part of Lincoln National Corp.)

Mary Todd Lincoln, 1861. (Courtesy of the Lincoln Museum, Fort Wayne, Indiana, a part of Lincoln National Corp.)

sions as his "public opinion baths." He conferred with members of his cabinet, with military officers, with his private secretaries; he studied maps and books on military tactics, read voluminous reports, and carried on extensive correspondence. If he took time for breakfast or lunch, the meals were light and quick and frequently taken as he worked. Around 4:00 P.M. he sometimes took a carriage ride with Mary, usually stopping to visit with sick and wounded soldiers in one of the always-crowded hospitals. After dinner he went back to his office and stayed until 11:00 P.M., then he often walked over to the War Department for the latest news. For relaxation he attended the theater, enjoyed the works of humorists satirizing the events of the time, and read the poetry and plays of William Shakespeare. According to one of his secretaries, he read more Shakespeare than all other writers combined. "I think nothing equals *Macbeth*," he told a Shakespearean actor. "It is wonderful."

Mary Todd Lincoln

For Mary, who as a girl had dreamed of being a president's wife, the years in the White House were not happy ones and they ended in horror. The wives of most previous presidents had been inconspicuous to the public and participated in formal entertainments as little as they could. But Mary intended to make the White House the center of Washington society, to play the role of "First Lady," and was the first president's wife to be so called. Naturally she encountered the hostility of Washington's pro-Southern society matrons, who derided her—as they did her husband—as a barely civilized westerner, though she was far better educated than most of them.

In accordance with her plans, Mary set about redecorating and refurnishing the White House, quickly exceeding the $20,000 Congress traditionally allowed for this purpose. When, apprehensively, she asked her husband to approve the excess bills and send them to Congress for payment, he angrily refused. Before asking for money *"for flub dubs for that damned old house,"* he told her, his voice rising, he would pay the bills himself.

Mary spent large sums on her personal wardrobe, although merchants in New York and Philadelphia sometimes lent her gowns to wear. The gowns, like those of the Empress Eugenie of France, who inspired them, featured the large hoop skirts favored by stout women, bare shoulders and arms, and low necklines, set off by simple but expensive jewelry. Elegance on such a grand scale was new to Washington and drew favorable comment. But there was much criticism, too, from those who believed that under the circumstances elegance was vulgar.

But Mary was allowed little time to enjoy the celebrity brought by her dinners and balls. On February 20, 1862, Willie Lincoln, now eleven, died of typhoid fever, and life was never again the same for her. Lincoln, too, was crushed by the death of his son, generally believed to be the brightest of all the Lincoln boys and the one most like his father, but he could not give way to his grief as Mary did to hers. Mary spent weeks in bed weeping, and when, later, heavily veiled in black, she attended the New York Avenue Presbyterian Church, she failed to find the solace she craved and turned to spiritualism.

The Lincolns usually spent the months from April to October in a cottage on the spacious and tree-shaded grounds of the Soldiers' Home outside Washington, the president commuting to the White House each day. Lonely and alone most of the time, Mary spent the summer of 1862 behind shuttered windows waiting for her husband's return and mourning for Willie. Convinced by spiritualists that only a thin veil separated her from her son, she often carried on conversations with him, and at least one seance was held in the cottage in an attempt to penetrate the veil; there were probably others in the White House. After about a year, Mary recovered from her shock and depression, but the joy had gone out of entertaining and she did much less of it.

In the meantime, she was being criticized for just about everything, for extravagance in the White House, for spending too much time mourning for Willie, for having so many close relatives fighting for the Confederacy, for the jealousy she often exhibited at receptions and reviews for women who were spending too much time with her husband. For the same reason, she seemed jealous of Lincoln's private secretaries, John G. Nicolay and John Hay, who referred to her as the "hell-cat." Even as a housewife in Springfield, Mary was known for temper tantrums and had had difficulty in holding on to servants. Now the strains of the endless war, the strains of being the wife of the much-attacked commander-in-chief, the strains of losing, in addition to Willie, three half-brothers and one brother-in-law in Confederate armies, the strains of being unpopular, the strains of having run up huge debts her husband knew nothing about became too much for her

Lincoln's summer residence, the Soldiers' Home. (Courtesy of the Lincoln Museum, Fort Wayne, Indiana, a part of Lincoln National Corp.)

unstable nervous temperament, and her abnormal behavior was sometimes acutely embarrassing to Lincoln. Yet the two also had their times of closeness.

Sitting beside her husband in Ford's Theatre that fatal night in April 1865, Mary slipped her hand into Lincoln's and, leaning close to him, whispered, "What will Miss Harris [a guest in the box] think of my hanging on to you so?" Lincoln answered her affectionately, "She won't think any thing about it."

Never again did Mary enter a theater. After five weeks of seclusion in her room at the White House, she began her widowhood as, years later, she ended it, mourning the loss of her husband and worrying about finances. Lincoln's estate, worth a substantial $80,000, was ample to pay off her debts, which included the price of eighty-five pairs of kid gloves bought just before the second inauguration and $3,200 in jewelry purchased in the three months before Ford's Theatre. The public sale of some of her clothing in New York brought public humiliation and very little cash, which was unneeded anyway. Traveling under false names, she and Tad went to Europe in 1868. Upon their return in 1871, Tad died, probably of tuberculosis.

Thanks to a pension granted by Congress and Tad's share of Lincoln's estate added to her own, she was a wealthy woman, but she remained obsessed with imagined poverty. Even so, periods of extreme frugality alternated with periods of irresponsible extravagance and other abnormalities like carrying $56,000 in government bonds sewn into her petticoats. In 1875 Robert Lincoln consulted old and trusted friends David Davis, the executor of Lincoln's estate, who had presided over the Eighth Judicial Circuit back in Illinois and been appointed by Lincoln to the U.S. Supreme Court, and John T. Stuart, Mary's cousin who had been Lincoln's first law partner. With their approval, Robert had his mother tried for insanity and committed to a private sanitarium in Batavia, Illinois. After four months, she was released to the custody of Ninian and Elizabeth Edwards in Springfield.

At a second trial in 1876 she was found to be sane, and after a trip to France returned to live until her death in 1882 with the Edwardses in the house in which she had been married. She remained in her room day and night with the shades drawn and a money belt around her waist and spent many hours going through her trunks fingering the fine cloth she had smuggled in from her last trip abroad.

Because of his near-total immersion in the military and political problems of the war, the loss of Willie, and the growing emotional imbalance of his wife, Lincoln did not have much of a family life in the White House. But he found a degree of compensatory satisfaction in his relations with four members of his official family.

The Official Family

Foremost in proximity and intimacy were private secretaries Nicolay, twenty-nine years old in 1861, and Hay, twenty-three. Both were like sons to Lincoln. They slept in a room directly opposite the president's office—though they took their meals mostly at Willard's Hotel—and Nicolay's office, which boasted one of the two water closets on the second floor of the White House, connected directly to the president's office. (The second water closet was at the other end of the building in the two-bedroom suite occupied by the Lincolns.)

Nicolay and Hay screened Lincoln's visitors, read and answered much of his mail, and prepared news summaries for his convenience. Often lying in bed late at night they would hear Lincoln shuffling in his bedroom slippers down the central corridor from his bedroom to theirs, his long and bony legs stretching ridiculously far below his nightshirt. Perhaps he carried a book to read to them, perhaps he simply wanted to tell stories and enjoy the relaxation of their company.

Nicolay and Hay revered Lincoln and, conscious of their closeness to the central figure in the most momentous era in American history, planned from the first to write a book about him. They took copious notes of his opinions and assessments of personalities, and Hay, in addition, kept a diary that provides an unparalleled look inside Lincoln's White House and his administration. Their ten-volume *Abraham Lincoln: A History*, based upon their notes and the huge collections of Lincoln's own papers, was published in 1890.

The ranking member of the cabinet was Secretary of State William H. Seward, who was bitterly disappointed when the presidential nomination in 1860 went to a man so much less experienced and qualified than he was. While Lincoln remained at home during the long months between his election and his inauguration, Seward was at work in the United States Senate, the Republican in charge, to the extent that anyone was. He expected to continue in charge after Lincoln's inauguration, running the government from the cabinet for a weak president, as had happened a number of times in the past. In fact, Seward even suggested to Lincoln in a memo dated April 1, 1861, that the president might want to put him in charge of policy formation. Lincoln promptly but smoothly, without rebuke, without giving offense, let Seward know that he was going to be in charge of his own administration. Very quickly, Seward learned that he had underestimated Lincoln. In June he wrote to his wife, "The President is the best of us."

The two men became good friends and often talked about their problems in a most informal manner, Seward lying on a couch in Lincoln's office smoking a cigar and Lincoln pacing back and forth, his hands clasped behind him. Seward was almost assassinated the evening of April 14, 1865, but recovered from his wounds and lived until 1872. On his tombstone in the cemetery at Auburn, New York, his home, is the epitaph "He was faithful." He was.

The fourth member of his official family with whom Lincoln enjoyed a warm personal relationship was Secretary of War Edwin M. Stanton. The two men first met in 1855 as co-defense attorneys in a major patent infringement case originally scheduled for trial in Chicago, where Lincoln had influence. But then the trial was switched to Cincinnati, where he had none. Stanton and another lawyer hired for the defense now had no use for the man from Illinois, who seemed to them an uncultured country lawyer competent only to argue cases about missing livestock and misplaced property lines. They were rude to him throughout the trial, in which he was an observer only, and Stanton, a Democrat, is said to have referred to him as a "giraffe" and a "damned long-armed ape." But Lincoln recognized Stanton as a man of great ability and was later impressed with his efforts as a member of President Buchanan's cabinet to strengthen the will of that faltering president during the secession crisis. Stanton was a staunch

John G. Nicolay, Lincoln, John Hay. (Courtesy of the Lincoln Museum, Fort Wayne, Indiana, a part of Lincoln National Corp.)

The attack on Secretary of State Seward, April 14, 1865. (From *Frank Leslie's Illustrated Magazine*, courtesy of the Lincoln Museum, Fort Wayne, Indiana, a part of Lincoln National Corp.)

Secretary of War Edwin M. Stanton, Lincoln's friend and closest associate. (Courtesy of the Lincoln Museum, Fort Wayne, Indiana, a part of Lincoln National Corp.)

Union man, and when Lincoln had to get rid of his first Secretary of War, Simon Cameron, for incompetence (or worse), he asked Stanton to take his place. Like Seward and so many others who had underestimated Lincoln by taking him, as it were, at face value, Stanton soon came to respect, admire, and love Lincoln.

Stanton was an easy man to dislike, for he was intense, hard-driving, opinionated, and quick-tempered, but there was a softness underneath that he revealed to few besides Lincoln. The two men sometimes took adjoining cottages at the Soldier's Home in the summer and rode back and forth together in deep discussions about the war. Seward was pretty much left to himself in the State Department, and Lincoln spent more time with Stanton than with any other official. One midnight, when Lincoln was heard climbing the stairs to the War Department telegraph office for news of his armies, someone heard Stanton tell the telegrapher to hide telegrams giving bad news and to find something favorable so that Lincoln would be able to sleep that night. The two men complemented each other. Lincoln tended to be soft-hearted and yielding and needed someone hard and inflexible, someone who could say no, to fall back upon.

After Lincoln's death, John Hay wrote to Stanton from Paris, "Not everyone knows, as I do, how close you stood to our lost leader, how he loved you and trusted you, and how vain were all the efforts to shake that trust and confidence, not lightly given and never withdrawn. All this will be known sometime of course, to his honor and yours."

Upon hearing of Stanton's death in 1869, Mary Lincoln took comfort from her conviction that history would record how nobly the secretary had served his country in its darkest hours. "My husband and himself," she told a friend, "were very warmly attached to each other and we can well believe, that they are *now* together—I do."

Instead of being generous to Stanton in recognition of his ceaseless struggle for the Union victory and his closeness to Lincoln, history has been unkind to him. It has stressed his mistakes and the abrasiveness of his personality and overlooked his monumental achievements as secretary of war. Lincoln's martyrdom is responsible, for the assassination has shielded the most controversial of all American presidents from the extremes of partisan attacks, leaving his closest associate exposed as the chief target of the long-lingering furies and resentments of the Civil War.

TWELVE

Northern Discord over Slavery

In prewar speeches Lincoln was careful to point out that his opposition to the spread of slavery into the western territories did not mean that he was opposed to the white people of the South. "They are just what we would be in their situation," he told his Northern audience. "If slavery did not now exist amongst them, they would not introduce it. If it did now exist amongst us, we should not instantly give it up." This historical perspective, this refusal to assume a position of moral superiority, is one of the things that made it possible for Lincoln, as president, to deal successfully with the problem of slavery.

The same historical perspective and refusal to assume moral superiority is required today if Americans are to understand why slavery, without which there could have been no Civil War, was so deep and complex a problem. To paraphrase Lincoln, we have to recognize that if we had been in the situation of the people of midnineteenth-century America we would have been just what they were then, not what we are now.

In an address in October 1864, Frederick Douglass, one of the most influential African-Americans in our history, declared that members of his race had to contend with two reactionary forces in American society. "The first and most powerful," he said, "is slavery; and the second, which may be said to be the shadow of slavery is prejudice against men because of their color." The chief agents of these two evil forces, he continued, were, first, the Democratic party and, second, the Republican party. "The Democratic party belongs to slavery; and the Republican party is largely under the power of prejudice against color." This is a point of view we cannot overlook. Even Republicans, members of a party whose stand against the spread of slavery had caused secession and whose leader had, by the time Douglass spoke, already declared free most of the slaves of the South, were prejudiced against blacks, free or slave. They were antislavery and antiblack at the same time. Between Republicans and Democrats there were fundamental disagreements about slavery and about whether the United States government should or could ever interfere with it, but members of both parties were prejudiced against blacks. They were divided over slavery but united in believing blacks to be inferior to themselves.

In the generation before the Civil War militant black and white abolitionists in the North denounced slavery and demanded its immediate abolition. But such individuals were only a small minority of the Northern population and were despised and feared by the majority. After the fighting began and the Union suffered one defeat after another in the East, the numbers and influence of abolitionists grew rapidly, for, as Lincoln said in his Second Inaugural Address, "all knew that . . . [slavery] was, somehow, the cause of the war." For the first time it became both respectable and patriotic to condemn slavery and advocate that it be destroyed so that it would never again disrupt the Union or cause a war. Of course these new recruits to abolition

or (to use the positive term coming into use) emancipation, were anti-Southern, antirebellion. There was no fundamental change in their attitude toward members of the
black race.

At the same time Republicans and many Northern
Democrats were becoming increasingly radical on the slavery issue, conservative proslavery sentiment in the North
not only remained strong but grew stronger as emancipation became a real possibility instead of merely an abstract
future threat. It had always been constitutional doctrine
that the United States had no authority over the internal
institutions of the states, and it is only natural that many
prominent and influential Northerners continued to believe it. Public opinion in the loyal slave states was vigor-
ously opposed to emancipation, as it was also in the South
and central parts of Ohio, Indiana, and Illinois. Workers
in the expanding industries of the North, many of them
impoverished immigrants, feared that emancipation would
bring about a massive migration of freed people to Northern cities, taking away jobs and housing. The controversy
over emancipation, in other words, divided the North just
as the controversy over slavery had divided the sections.

The problem of slavery as it confronted Lincoln was
that if he yielded to the growing demands from Republicans to take action against slavery, he would further alienate the border states, possibly driving one or more of them
into the Confederacy, stimulate anti-administration and
antiwar feeling throughout the North, and run the risk of
sabotage, riots, and major or minor public uprisings. On
the other hand, if he failed to act, he would lose control
of his own party and the Northern war effort would likely
collapse in the futility of angry recriminations.

Although Lincoln had been pondering this problem for months, it was the failure of General McClellan's campaign against Richmond early in July 1862 that convinced him emancipation had become a military necessity. Simultaneously, the general's attitude convinced him it was a political necessity as well, for in the letter he handed the president at Harrison's Landing on July 8 he stated positively that no change should be made in the conduct of war. "Neither confiscation of property . . . or forcible abolition of slavery should be contemplated for a moment." Such sentiments made it clear that McClellan was assuming leadership of the conservatives of the North and would likely be Lincoln's opponent in the next presidential election.

The time had come for Lincoln to put himself at the head of the North's radicals. Later the same month, he read his draft of the emancipation policy to his cabinet, explaining that his mind was made up about emancipation but that he was asking for reactions. The reactions were mostly favorable, but Secretary of State Seward observed that coming so soon after McClellan's defeat in the Seven Days' battle, Lincoln's proclamation seemed like an act of desperation, a "cry for help." Lincoln was conscious of the importance of timing in the adoption of so radical a policy and knew good advice when he heard it. So he put the proclamation aside for a more positive occasion.

In the meantime, radical leaders, not knowing that Lincoln had decided to adopt the policy of emancipation, continued to criticize him for failing to adopt it. On August 20, Horace Greeley, one of the most influential newspaper editors, published in his *New York Tribune* what he called "The Prayer of Twenty Millions." Greeley was disappointed by Lincoln's "do-nothing" policy on slavery.

"We think you are unduly influenced by the counsels . . . of certain fossil politicians from the Border Slave States. . . . On the face of this wide earth, Mr. President, there is not one disinterested, determined, intelligent champion of the Union cause who does not feel that all attempts to put down the Rebellion and at the same time uphold its inciting cause are preposterous and futile."

Instead of assuring Greeley that he agreed with him and that he was going to issue a proclamation freeing slaves, Lincoln took advantage of the opportunity to educate the public toward acceptance of the radical policy he was about to adopt. Prejudiced moderates and conservatives who would oppose emancipation if presented as an end in itself might be willing to accept it as a means of preserving the Union and ending the war. "My paramount object in this struggle," he said to such people in his reply to Greeley, reprinted in most other Northern newspapers, "*is* to save the Union, and is *not* either to save or to destroy slavery. If I could save the Union without freeing *any* slave, I would do it, and if I could save it by freeing *all* the slaves I would do it; and if I could save it by freeing some and leaving others alone I would also do that. What I do about slavery . . . , I do because I believe it helps to save the Union; and what I forebear, I forebear because I do *not* believe it would help to save the Union." Lincoln concluded this brilliantly crafted letter by stating it gave his view of his *official* duty. "I intend no modification of my oft-expressed *personal* wish that all men everywhere could be free."

On September 17, McClellan stopped Lee's invasion of the North at Antietam, Maryland, and the strategic victory gave Lincoln the chance to announce his radical change of policy on slavery. In what is known as the Preliminary Emancipation Proclamation, dated September 22, 1862, Lincoln declared that any Southern state that stopped fighting and agreed to a program of gradual emancipation with compensation to the owners would be considered no longer in rebellion against the United States. On January 1, he would issue another proclamation freeing all the slaves in the states and parts of states that were then still in rebellion.

Lincoln did not really expect any Southern state to accept these terms, but moderates and conservatives would have to concede that he had given the South an alternative to radical emancipation.

THIRTEEN

Emancipation

The Emancipation Proclamation of January 1, 1863, declared free all the slaves in those parts of the South at war with the United States. Where did the president get the power to free them? In his Inaugural Address, March 4, 1861, he had said, "I have no purpose, directly or indirectly, to interfere with the institution of slavery in the States where it exists. I believe I have no lawful right to do so, and I have no inclination to do so." When he made that statement the United States was at peace; now it was at war. Lincoln believed that as commander-in-chief of the army and navy during war he could free slaves as legally as he could confiscate any other property. The proclamation was issued, in its own words, "as a fit and necessary war measure for suppressing . . . rebellion." Since the border slave states and certain recaptured areas of the South were not at war with the United States, Lincoln's war powers did not extend to them and their slaves were therefore unaffected. Slavery everywhere in the United States was ended by the Thirteenth Amendment passed by Congress early in 1865, thanks to powerful political pressures applied by Lincoln. It was ratified in December.

Some Americans today are inclined to take the Emancipation Proclamation for granted and to wonder why Lincoln was so slow in issuing it. But at the time it did more than any other single act to arouse hatred for Lincoln and opposition to his war. The Democrats, who controlled the legislature of Lincoln's own state, denounced it "as an ineffaceable disgrace to the American people." Other Northern states also condemned it as unconstitutional and as a betrayal of the original purpose of the war. General McClellan wrote his wife that, along with other of Lincoln's incompetencies, emancipation makes it "almost impossible for me to retain my commission & self respect at the same time." Former Democratic president of the United States Franklin Pierce announced that the Emancipation Proclamation showed that Lincoln was now, "to the extent of his limited ability and narrow intelligence," the willing tool of the abolitionists. Jefferson Davis called the proclamation "the most execrable measure recorded in the history of guilty man."

Virulent prejudice against blacks was the fundamental reason for opposition to the proclamation. The editor of an extreme anti-Lincoln magazine published in New York warned that unless Lincoln and the other abolitionist traitors were stopped, the United States would become "a mongrel concern of whites, negroes, mulattoes, and sambos, . . . the most degrading and contemptible the world ever saw." For that reason, no patriotic citizen could rejoice at news of a Union victory. The American people recognized that Jefferson Davis's government was a thousand times closer to the spirit of the Founders than that of "Abraham Africanus I."

In March 1863 Lincoln told a radical Congressman that he thought the Proclamation had done about as much harm in the North as good. But soon he came to believe that the good outweighed the harm, that emancipation, admittedly a gamble, had paid off. To one group of conservatives who complained that he had sold out to the abolitionists, Lincoln replied, the "war is & will be carried on so long as I am President, for the sole purpose of restoring the Union. But no human power can subdue this rebellion without using the Emancipation lever as I have done."

The emancipation lever worked in several ways. Among upper-class New England and New York intellectuals, it gave the war new nobility. Many of these men and women were not much moved by Lincoln's war for democracy, for popular, republican government. After all, it meant the transfer of political power from themselves to an uneducated majority. But ending slavery was something they could rejoice over, and did. Many members of the general public also felt a lift at the realization that the federal government would use its power to end the institution. After the proclamation, only the North could convincingly identify its cause with that of humanity. The North's war began as a war for self-preservation and ended as a war for freedom; the South's war began as a war for freedom and ended as a war for self-preservation. The exchange of moral leverage is obvious.

Above all, the Emancipation Proclamation put at Lincoln's disposal 180,000 African-American soldiers—the equivalent of nearly two armies of the Potomac—without whose help Lincoln said repeatedly he could not subdue the rebellion.

FOURTEEN

Hostility in the North for Lincoln and His War

When Lincoln changed the object of the war from preserving the Union to preserving the Union by freeing the slaves, he lost the support of many people in the North and border states who were willing to fight for their country but not for the "niggers." But since the president had established emancipation as a military necessity undertaken to win the war, it was difficult for them to attack the proclamation directly. Instead, they increased their condemnation of Lincoln personally as a dictator who cared nothing for constitutional restraints on his power. He was vulnerable to the charge, for he had exercised far more executive power than any other president of the United States before or since. At the beginning of the war he delayed calling Congress into special session and proceeded to act on his own initiative. By executive decree he raised and spent large sums of money, called out the state militia, and increased the size of the army and navy, though the Constitution gives power to do these things to Congress alone. He suspended the writ of habeas corpus in the area of Washington, D.C., making civilians subject to military arrest and trial, another power belonging exclusively to Congress according to the Chief Justice of the U.S. Supreme Court. When it assembled, Congress gave these and other actions its retroactive approval, but most Democrats and many Republicans made no secret of their strong opposition to such presidential usurpations.

On September 24, 1862, two days after his Preliminary Emancipation Proclamation brought such a radical change in the object and conduct of the war, Lincoln issued another proclamation. He announced that all persons resisting the draft, discouraging enlistments in the army or encouraging desertions, or guilty of "any disloyal practice affording aid and comfort to Rebels" would be subject to martial law and military trial. By war's end, many thousands of civilians—mostly in the border states—were in fact arrested by the military and held in prison with or without military trials. How could there fail to be the most vigorous denunciation of a president responsible for such actions?

Lincoln's most extreme enemies in the North were called Copperheads by Republicans, after the poisonous snake. The Copperheads saw themselves very differently, of course. In standing against Lincoln's tyranny and his unjust war, they believed they were the truly loyal Americans. Many of them cut the head of "Liberty" from the large copper penny in circulation and wore it proudly wherever it was safe to do so, as it was, for example, on the streets of Springfield, Illinois. Manufacturers offered Copperhead pins for sale, advertising that "Every person in favor of Free Speech, a Free Press and the Rights of White men, is wearing the Badge of Liberty." A Copperhead editor in New York asked his readers in 1863, "Which do we prefer—to let the South go, or to lose our own liberties in an attempt to force it unwillingly into a union with us?"

Copperheads railed self-righteously against emancipation and conscription; they encouraged soldiers to desert and gave refuge to many who did; they engaged in acts of sabotage and acted as spies and smugglers; they conspired against the government with Confederate agents, who slipped easily back and forth across the border or entered the United States from Canada, where there was an active Confederate mission.

The best-known Copperhead leader was Clement L. Vallandigham, a Democratic member of Congress from Ohio, who vehemently opposed all the measures taken by Lincoln to win the war: the ruthless force being used against the South, which ended all hope of reunion; the suspension of habeas corpus and the subjection of civilians suspected of disloyal acts to military law and imprisonment; and the emancipation of slaves. "Time will but burn the memory of these wrongs deeper into our hearts," he exclaimed in the House of Representatives. "Let us expel the usurper and restore the Constitution and laws, the rights of the states, and the liberties of the people."

In May 1863, General Burnside, now commanding the Department of Ohio, arrested Vallandigham for expressing "treasonable sympathy" with the enemy and put him in a cell in Cincinnati. From prison Vallandigham issued a statement: "I am a Democrat—for the Constitution, for law, for the Union, for liberty—this is my only 'crime.' In obedience to the demands of Northern abolition disunionists and traitors, I am here in bonds today."

Democrats all across the North and some concerned Republicans, too, rushed to Vallandigham's defense. In a

Lincoln in November 1863. Note his upward-roving left eye. (Courtesy of the Lincoln Museum, Fort Wayne, Indiana, a part of Lincoln National Corp.)

speech on July 4, former president Pierce declared that the Lincoln administration was telling the people that "in time of war the mere arbitrary will of the President takes the place of the Constitution, and the President himself announces to us that it is treasonable to speak or to write otherwise than as he may prescribe."

Vallandigham was tried in a military court and sentenced to two years in a military prison. But Lincoln had not approved the Copperhead leader's arrest and feared that making a martyr of him would only strengthen the antiwar opposition. He therefore commuted the sentence to banishment within the Confederacy. Vallandigham soon ran the blockade and from Canada entered the race for governor of Ohio. He was defeated by a war Democrat running with Republican support, but nevertheless polled 35 percent of the vote. Privately Lincoln was disturbed that any "genuine American" could have voted for Vallandigham, and one out of every three Ohio voters had, even though the candidate had been out of the country. The North was truly at war against itself, and in 1864 it was by no means certain who would win, Unionists or antiwar Democrats.

Nor was it certain whether Unionists or Confederates would win it in the South. Lincoln had long urged his generals to coordinate their operations in the eastern and western theaters, but no such grand strategy was put into effect until Grant became general-in-chief. In the West, Grant assigned William Tecumseh Sherman the task of capturing and destroying railroads and centers of communications—with the major target being Atlanta, Georgia—so that help could not be sent to the East, where Grant set out to destroy Lee's army. In what became a war of attrition, Grant pounded Lee in bloody battles—the Wilderness, Spotsylvania, Cold Harbor—losing more troops in his offensive operations than Lee had available to him for defense. Public opinion in the North was appalled at the slaughter and Grant was denounced as a butcher. But even in losing a good part of his army, so much larger than Lee's, he knew he would ultimately overwhelm his adversary and win the war, unless the people of the North refused to pay the price of victory. In June 1864 he adopted a plan of operations similar to what McClellan had attempted in 1862, transporting his army down Chesapeake Bay and up the James River and laying siege to Petersburg, twenty miles south of Richmond. To many discouraged Northerners it looked as if a bloody and endless stalemate would be the only result.

In the West Sherman made only slow progress in his move against Atlanta from his base in Chattanooga, Tennessee.

A Confederate army under Jubal A. Early, in the meantime, had cleared Union forces out of the Shenandoah Valley of Virginia—Richmond's breadbasket—and headed northward toward Washington and Baltimore. There was panic in both cities. "Let us . . . keep cool," Lincoln pleaded with a mayors' committee in Baltimore on July 10. "I hope neither Baltimore nor Washington will be sacked." The *London Times* reported that "the Confederacy is more formidable as an enemy than ever." And this after three years and three months of war.

On July 11 Early was stopped within sight of Washington and, in fact, within sight of Lincoln, who observed the fighting from Fort Stevens on the capital's northern defense perimeter. But later in the month, Early marched northward again and burned the city of Chambersburg, Pennsylvania.

The Battle of Gettysburg is often referred to as the "high tide of the Confederacy." The summer of 1864 may be accurately described as the "low tide of the Union." Bankers had so little confidence in the prospects for victory that the government had to pay 15 percent to borrow funds. When Lincoln was forced to issue a proclamation on July 18 calling for 500,000 volunteers, the response was so poor that a draft had to be scheduled for September, very bad timing indeed with the presidential election coming up. One of Lincoln's confidential advisers on politics told the president he faced certain defeat. Despite heartbreaking casualties, he had failed to subdue the rebellion, and the people of the North were wild for peace. "Our only hope," wrote Anna Ridgely in Springfield, Illinois, "is in a Democratic President, or an uprising of the people to demand their rights as free men."

FIFTEEN

Reelection in 1864

As expected the Democrats nominated General McClellan as their candidate for president and adopted a platform—written by Clement L. Vallandigham, now back in the United States and attempting vainly to be rearrested—calling for an immediate cessation of hostilities, followed by a convention to bring about the peaceful reunion of North and South. As a warrior Democrat, McClellan knew that a cease-fire would lead not to reunion but to independence for the Confederacy, and so he repudiated this part of the platform. As president, he announced he would continue to fight. But it was unlikely that either his party or his own views on warfare would permit him to fight the brutal kind of war that alone could bring victory. In a confidential memorandum on August 23, Lincoln wrote that it seemed probable his administration would not be reelected. In that case, he said, "It will be my duty to so cooperate with the President elect, as to save the Union between the election and the inauguration; as he will have secured his election on such ground that he cannot possibly save it afterwards."

But the tide had already turned in favor of the Union. Earlier in August Admiral David Farragut damned the torpedoes and captured Mobile Bay, Alabama, closing one of the Confederacy's few remaining major harbors. On September 2 Sherman's army captured Atlanta, and suddenly it looked as if the war was not such a failure, after all. Lincoln, who knew how to play good cards when he got them, ordered the celebration of these victories by the firing of one-hundred-gun salutes at Washington, New York, Boston, Philadelphia, Baltimore, Pittsburgh, St. Louis, and other politically important cities and proclaimed a day of national Thanksgiving.

Maine and Vermont held their elections in September and voted Republican by large majorities. Still the Republicans, or as they called themselves in this election, the Unionists, expected a close election and therefore made sure that soldiers, overwhelmingly pro-Union, would be able to vote in the field. They also hastened to admit scantily populated Nevada into the Union as the thirty-sixth state in order to count its electoral votes. In addition, they sought to discredit the Democratic opposition as disloyal by giving extensive publicity to the trial of some Copperhead leaders for treason before a military commission in Indianapolis, Indiana, and by releasing a War Department report greatly exaggerating the dangers of a vast, organized, and armed Copperhead uprising.

It turned out to be a landslide victory for Lincoln, who received 55 percent of the popular vote, the highest percentage given any president between Andrew Jackson and Theodore Roosevelt. Not only was the election a personal satisfaction to Lincoln, it vindicated the democratic principle for which he was fighting: it proved that the people were capable of governing themselves even under the most perverse circumstances. "It has demonstrated," Lincoln told a crowd of serenaders on the White House lawn, "that a people's government can sustain a national election in the midst of a great civil war. Until now it has not been known to the world that this was a possibility."

SIXTEEN

The Anti-Lincoln Reaction:
John Wilkes Booth

If the election was a victory for popular government and the continued prosecution of the war, it was a devastating blow for the Confederates and Copperheads who so recently had had such good reason to believe the North would vote for peace. Since it had not, it was natural that some of those who most hated Lincoln and who most ardently embraced the righteousness of the Confederate cause should have believed the time had come to take direct political action against the enemy leader chiefly responsible for the impending defeat of everything they believed in. One such hater of Lincoln and devotee of the Southern cause was John Wilkes Booth. A popular young actor and member of a prominent theatrical family, Booth was born on a Maryland farm and raised in Baltimore, a city that probably counted more pro-Confederates than any city in the Confederacy. In Maryland and in the Northern cities in which he played as a star, Booth associated with other Copperheads, who were most numerous in the cities, and came into contact with some of the many Southern agents in the North. There is evidence that he was himself a Southern agent, a spy who smuggled medi-

cine and information into the South. Late in the summer
of 1864 he became involved in one of several known conspiracies to capture Lincoln. During one of his unescort-
ed drives to or from his cottage at the Soldier's Home,
Booth would seize him and rush him by relays of fast horses through the pro-Confederate countryside of southern
Maryland to a waiting boat on the Potomac at Port Tobacco, some thirty miles away. Once across the river into
Virginia, the captive president would be escorted to Richmond and held hostage for the release of Confederate prisoners of war or other perhaps decisive concessions. In
November, after the presidential election, Booth went to
Montreal, discussed the plan—which was both feasible and
legitimate as an act of war—with the Confederate representatives there, and shipped his theatrical wardrobe to
Richmond, where he hoped to join it and use it. Upon returning to Washington, he organized a group of like-mind-
ed friends to help him and scouted out the region through
which he hoped to transport Lincoln. Weeks and months
slipped away without offering Booth a reasonable opportunity to carry out his plan successfully. On March 17,
1865, when such an opportunity did seem to present itself, it came to nothing.

The Union war effort was now fast approaching its vic-
torious conclusion. Sherman had marched from Atlanta to
the sea, laying waste a large swath of Georgia as he went,
and was heading northward through the Carolinas, slowed
down by the delaying tactics of a Confederate army under
Joseph E. Johnston. The Confederate government fled from
Richmond on April 2, just before the fall of Petersburg
would have left it trapped in its own capital, and the next
day Union forces occupied both cities. Lincoln himself vis-

John Wilkes Booth. (Courtesy of the Lincoln Museum, Fort Wayne, Indiana, a part of Lincoln National Corp.)

ited Richmond on April 4 and Petersburg on the eighth (he had been in the latter city briefly on the third), receiving in both places a tumultuous welcome from the people he had freed. He returned to Washington on April 9, the same day that Lee surrendered to Grant at Appomattox.

For days there had been wild rejoicing throughout the North, but nowhere was there greater unrestrained joy than at the White House on April 10, where a large crowd had spent the day singing patriotic songs and calling for Lincoln. Finally the president appeared at a second-story window above the north entrance, where he had often before spoken to crowds. After acknowledging the people's cheers and promising to give them a speech the next evening, he made a startling request. He asked one of the bands to play "Dixie," the Rebel anthem. It seemed strange to hear the president of the United States call for that tune, but then the crowd recognized it was a sign the war was over, that Southerners were no longer their enemies. When the band finished, it struck up "Yankee Doodle," Lincoln remaining at the window. Then he called for three cheers for General Grant and his soldiers and three more for the gallant navy and bowed away. Most of the people hurried off to serenade Stanton at the War Department.

In the speech he promised for the evening of April 11 and which he delivered from the same upstairs window, Lincoln spoke about the complex issues of Reconstruction, issues that divided the people of the North just as the issues of the war had. In his Second Inaugural Address the previous month, Lincoln had pledged himself to a peace of "malice toward none . . . , charity for all," and he wanted to make it as easy as possible for the Southern states to resume their old positions within the Union under new, loyal governments. Yet the federal government would have to take some kind of action, unprecedented in the past, to assure that the people freed by the Emancipation Proclamation actually got their freedom and were not returned to some kind of servitude. As a first step, Lincoln now told his audience that he thought literate black men and those who had served in the army should be enfranchised. Many Republicans thought this action was not radical enough, but most Democrats found the suggestion revolting. One of the latter was John Wilkes Booth, who was standing near enough to the window to hear Lincoln's words. Angrily, he turned to a companion. "That means nigger citizenship," he said. "Now, by God, I'll put him through. That is the last speech he will ever make."

SEVENTEEN

April 14, 1865

After his April 9 return to Washington from two and a half weeks with Grant's army, Lincoln scarcely had a moment to himself. John Hay was on hand to talk over daily plans, but Nicolay had left for Charleston, South Carolina, to represent the president at ceremonies to be held at Fort Sumter on April 14 commemorating the end of the war at the place where it had started precisely four years before. Then began, for the next few days, an endless series of conferences with Seward and Stanton and other members of his administration, with high-ranking military and naval officers, with members of Congress, and with officials from the states. Some of the visitors, preoccupied with Reconstruction policies, advised Lincoln that he must take stronger steps to assure that former Rebel leaders did not continue in political power in their states, or that more vigorous action must be taken to protect Southern blacks from reprisals by Southern whites. Most of the whites were emotionally unable to accept that those who had been their private property were now free men and women. Others warned him that for the federal government to interfere in such matters, previously left up to the states, amounted to a continuation of wartime despotism and represented an obstacle to reunion. Always there were favor-seekers

The last photograph taken of Lincoln, February 5, 1865.
(Courtesy of the Lincoln Museum, Fort Wayne, Indiana, a
part of Lincoln National Corp.)

waiting to press their cases, mothers, perhaps, beseeching the president for clemency for sons guilty of violations of military discipline or politicians seeking jobs for relatives or constituents. One after another they lay siege to his office and, as always, he listened to their entreaties, usually with patience, sometimes with resignation, occasionally with irritation. He was a weary man—even the constant chorus of congratulations became wearisome—but he was unspeakably grateful that the killing was almost over and that the nation and the principle of democratic government would not perish from the earth.

His son Robert, who had served briefly on Grant's staff and had been present at Lee's surrender, joined him for breakfast on April 14 and gave him a firsthand account of the historic scene at Appomattox. At a three-hour cabinet meeting his spirits were high, even though most of the discussion dealt with problems of Reconstruction, which were proving to be more difficult and complex in fact than they had seemed, earlier, in theory. Perhaps his good mood was influenced by the dream he had had the night before. He dreamed that he was aboard an indescribable vessel of some kind heading at great speed toward an indefinite shore, a dream that had come to him several times during the war before a major event, usually a Union victory. This time he thought it must signify that Sherman had fought and won a battle against Johnston in North Carolina and that there would be no more fighting. He conferred with his new vice-president, Andrew Johnson, in midafternoon, and later took a drive with Mary in an open carriage.

Mary Lincoln remembered that he was almost boyish in his cheerfulness as they drove along the Potomac, reminding her of how he had been in the carefree days in

Springfield when he was surrounded only by people who loved him. When she remarked upon his playfulness, he told her he considered the war to have ended that very day. They both must try to be more cheerful in the future, he said. At dinner he spoke of being tired and of looking forward to seeing the comedy *Our American Cousin* playing at Ford's Theatre. He was eager to escape the White House and its never-ending visitors and demands. He wanted relaxation. He wanted to laugh.

The audience's laughter at a funny line of dialogue was the last sound he ever heard.

"Sic Semper Tyrannis!"—thus always to tyrants—cried John Wilkes Booth after firing the shot into the back of Lincoln's head and vaulting from the presidential box to the stage below. In front of the uncomprehending audience he held aloft a dagger dripping with the blood of Major Henry R. Rathbone, a guest of the Lincolns' who had tried to seize him. On the dagger, now on display in a glass case at the theater, are inscribed the words "America Land of the Free Home of the Brave Liberty Independance [*sic*]." Then he hurried upstage as fast as the leg he had broken in his jump would allow and exited through the rear door to a waiting horse. Twelve days later, after the biggest manhunt in American history, he was tracked to a farm in Virginia and shot by a United States soldier as, heavily armed, he sought to limp his way out of a flaming tobacco shed. He died a few hours later. Among his last words were, "Tell mother I die for my country."

Lincoln's inert body was carried from the theater across the street to a tiny back bedroom in a boardinghouse kept

The President's box at Ford's Theatre showing the U.S. Treasury flag that caused Booth to lose his balance and break his leg when jumping to the stage. (Courtesy of the Lincoln Museum, Fort Wayne, Indiana, a part of Lincoln National Corp.)

Ford's Theatre. (Courtesy Civil War Collection, Special Collections, San Diego State University Library)

The house where Lincoln died. (Courtesy Civil War Collection, Special Collections, San Diego State University Library)

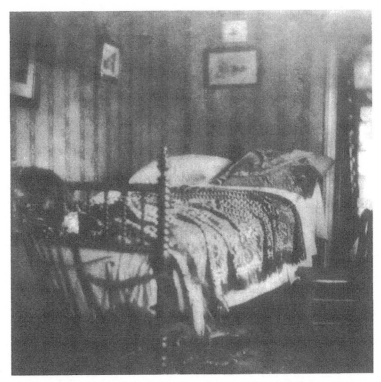

Lincoln's deathbed. (Courtesy of the Lincoln Museum, Fort Wayne, Indiana, a part of Lincoln National Corp.)

by one William Petersen, where doctors made the dying president as comfortable as possible. Recognizing the wound as mortal, there was nothing else they could do.

The news of the shooting of Lincoln and the vicious knife attack on Secretary Seward as he lay in his bed at home, which occurred at about the same time, spread rapidly throughout the city, along with a nightmarish terror that still other leaders might become the victims of what was assumed to be a massive conspiracy of Rebels and Copperheads. From a back parlor close to where Lincoln lay, Stanton ordered guards around the homes of prominent officials and alerted all those military commanders around Washington he could reach by telegraph to be on the lookout for the escaping assassins. Despite the possibility of danger, Robert Lincoln, John Hay, cabinet members, and other political leaders, including the soon-to-be president, Andrew Johnson, converged upon the Petersen house. After saying their silent good-byes to the president and talking quietly amongst themselves, most of them moved on to make room for others. Some—Robert, Hay, Stanton, Secretary Welles, Senator Charles Sumner, the doctors—stayed by the bedside all night.

Mary Lincoln, her dress stained by Major Rathbone's blood—which she believed to be that of her husband—and made delirious by this new and sudden agony, spent the night being cared for by friends in the front parlor. Occasionally, with assistance, she made her way to the back bedroom, kissed her husband repeatedly and pleaded with him not to die. But he did die—at 7:22 Saturday morning, April 15—and the news of his death stunned the nation.

EIGHTEEN

Democracy's Martyr

The thirteen-day journey that took Lincoln's body back to Springfield contrasted tragically with the journey of 1861. Now there was no cheering and no bands arousing patriotic emotions. Instead, there were black-draped cities and citizens, memorial services, hymns, eulogies, and the solemn sound of muffled drums.

The slow-moving train stopped at nine cities where Lincoln's casket was removed from its special car and taken through crowds of mourners to a place suitable for public viewing. The first of these cities was Baltimore, where in 1861 it had been too dangerous for Lincoln to show his face. Thousands of citizens solemnly filed past the open casket, now resting on a catafalque surrounded by flowers, and looked through tear-filled eyes at the features of their dead president. If there were still Lincoln-haters in Baltimore and New York and the other cities—and of course there were—they were smart enough to keep quiet, so quiet that Americans soon forgot they had ever existed.

The last of Lincoln's many funerals, attended by thousands, took place outdoors at Springfield's Oak Ridge Cemetery on May 4, 1865. But Lincoln's body did not rest in peace. In 1876 an attempt was made to steal it and hold it for ransom. While extensive modifications were made

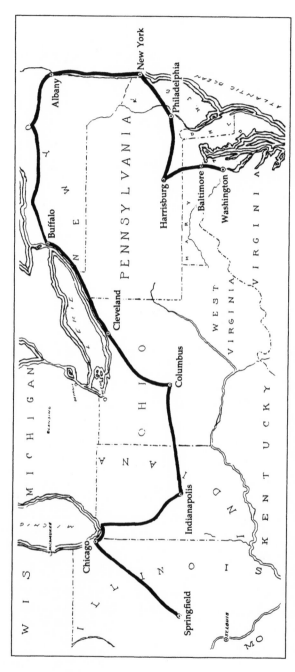

The major stops of Lincoln's funeral train, Washington, D.C., to Springfield, April 21–May 3, 1865

in the construction of the tomb, the coffin was secretly moved from place to place within it and around it. Finally, in 1901, with the rebuilding completed, the casket was lifted from an outside vault, opened for the last time, and the well-preserved remains identified. It was then placed within a sunken vault near the coffins of his wife and three deceased sons and covered with two tons of concrete.

A large part of the lasting impact of Lincoln's death has been due to its timing, to the brutal suddenness with which it terminated the joyous celebrations taking place all across the Northern states. In an instant, jubilation and the yearning for national reconciliation carefully cultivated by Lincoln in his Second Inaugural Address were transformed into grief and blazing anger against Southerners and Copperheads. The grief persisted, but the anger faded away when it appeared that Booth and his small group of friends—not leading Rebels and Copperheads—had been solely responsible for the assassination.

His martyrdom has blinded Americans to the hatred felt for Lincoln by so many of his compatriots during the war. Yet recognition that the hatred was very real and very widespread in both sections—and that it was not without rational basis—provides important insights into the terrible nature of the war. Removing the assassination from the context of its times and blaming it exclusively on Booth's mean-spirited character or moral depravity helped to make possible the reunion of the North and the South, but it has distorted the history of the Civil War.

The half million city dwellers who stood in lines for hours to see Lincoln lying in state for seconds, and another half million Americans in small towns and the open countryside who stood in all weather and at all hours patiently waiting

Lying in state in Chicago. (From *Harper's Weekly*, courtesy of the Lincoln Museum, Fort Wayne, Indiana, a part of Lincoln National Corp.)

Lincoln tomb reconstruction, showing Lincoln's casket being lifted from a temporary vault for permanent entombment.
(Courtesy of the Illinois State Historical Library)

to see the funeral train pass slowly by, were united in their sense of loss and love. In essence, if not in intensity, this emotional attachment to Lincoln has been felt by members of every subsequent generation. It has elevated our most controversial president to a level above controversy.

But just as oversimplifying the assassination by blaming it on evil in the assassin misrepresents history, so does the opposite extreme of thinking and speaking of Lincoln as if he were some kind of divinity. Lincoln was no god and would not like being thought of as one. He was, rather, an extraordinary human being, whose unpretentious leadership, gifts of persuasion, and selfless dedication to the democratic ideal enabled him to guide the nation to victory in a war against itself. He saved the American experiment in popular government and thus gave future generations the chance to spread and deepen democracy and, as he put it, increase "the happiness and value of life to all people of all colors everywhere."

NINETEEN

Lincoln the War Leader

Toward the end of the war Lincoln told a friend, "I claim not to have controlled events, but confess plainly that events have controlled me." But he was being characteristically modest. Of course he had no absolute control over events; no one ever has had, and no one ever will. Even when we human beings do not sow the wind, we have to reap the whirlwind: we have to deal with the problems of our times even though we have not created them. During a whirlwind like the Civil War it was an incredible achievement in political leadership for Lincoln to keep the North right side up and in the war. The poet Walt Whitman recognized it. Lincoln "has shown, I sometimes think," Whitman wrote in 1863, "an almost supernatural tact in keeping the ship afloat at all, with head steady—not only not going down— . . . but with proud and resolute spirit, and flag waving in sight of the world, menacing and high as ever. I say never yet captain, never yet ruler, had such a perplexing dangerous task as his."

After an interview with Lincoln in 1864, one man wrote in his diary that he felt he had "stood in the presence of the great guiding intellect of the age." "He mastered and directed public sentiment upon the most vital questions," said another. "Mr. Lincoln has exerted a greater influence upon the popular heart and in forming public opinion than any man," declared a member of Congress.

Lincoln was a great war leader because he was able to reach the hearts and minds of enough people to win the war. Who could have done more? How easy it would have been to do less. Lincoln did not wipe out; he rode the big wave; he weathered the hurricane.

Lincoln's successful leadership was not a matter of blind luck, and certainly not merely a matter of the North's superiority over the South in resources and numbers of soldiers. Lincoln understood the crucial importance of public opinion in a democracy. "Public opinion in this country," he said truly, "is everything." "Any policy to be permanent must have public opinion at the bottom." He was able to shape or influence public opinion on the vital issues because he wrote and spoke with clarity and precision and used language, rich in metaphors, the people understood. Often—too often, many associates thought—he illustrated a point or dealt with a delicate situation by drawing upon his inexhaustible supply of stories. "I have found in the course of long experience," he explained to a prominent New Yorker, that people "are more easily influenced and informed through the medium of a broad illustration than in any other way, and as to what the hypercritical few may think, I don't care." Lincoln was a successful war leader because he knew the people he was leading, knew how to communicate with them and help them understand why victory was worth the ghastly sacrifices he was asking of them. Just as surely as most people are born followers, Lincoln was a born leader.

Many bloody battles had to be fought and lost before it was recognized that the South could only be defeated by abandoning the restrictive practices of limited warfare, a lesson Lincoln learned before the nation's professionally trained generals, except Grant. As commander-in-chief, he applied himself endlessly to his responsibilities. William Russell, the correspondent of the *London Times*, described him early in the war "trying with all his might to understand strategy, naval warfare, big guns, the movement of troops, military maps, reconnaissances, occupations, interior and exterior lines, and all the technical details of the art of slaying. He runs from one house to another, armed with plans, papers, reports, recommendations, sometimes good-humored, never angry, occasionally dejected, and always a little fussy." He never stopped thinking and studying about how to win the war, and he was intensely interested in new weapons and improved explosives. Often he had to struggle against conservative and unimaginative ordinance officers to get new arms and armament adopted.

"Intelligent understanding" was one of Lincoln's chief characteristics, believed an assistant secretary of war. "You felt that here was a man who saw through things, who understood, and you respected him accordingly." Lincoln had the ability, said an English observer during the war, to see two sides to every controversy. This ability might leave him in occasional doubt about the wisdom of a particular decision or policy, but he was nevertheless a man of decision. "It is my duty to hear all," he told the head of a delegation complaining about problems emancipation was bringing in the West, "but at last I must . . . judge what to do and what to forebear."

Who else but a man who could see two sides to every controversy but understood that when it was time for a decision he was the one who had to make it could have held so many of the diverse and antagonistic factions of the divided North together? "The Tycoon is in fine whack," wrote John Hay in his diary. "I have rarely seen him more serene and busy. He is managing this war, the draft, foreign relations, and planning a reconstruction of the Union all at once." And later he added: "The old man sits here and wields like a backwoods Jupiter the bolts of war and the machinery of government with a hand equally steady & equally firm." "I believe," Hay told a friend, "he will fill a bigger place in history than he even dreams of himself."

Lincoln was a successful war leader, too, because he understood that the leader of a badly fractured section within a divided nation had to occupy a position in the middle. "I hope to 'stand firm' enough to not go backward," he wrote a leading Senator, "and yet not go forward . . . [so fast as to] wreck the country's cause." To a general trying to maintain an uneasy peace between feuding Unionists in Missouri, he advised, "if both factions, or neither, shall abuse you, you will probably be about right. Beware of being assailed by one, and praised by the other."

Lincoln led from the middle and was thus vulnerable to abuse from all sides: from conservative Republicans and radical Republicans, from war Democrats and peace Democrats, from Copperheads and Rebels, from border slave states and abolitionist states, and from dozens of lesser groups and interests all wishing him to be more responsive to their needs and less solicitous of those of others. (So it has been ever since with special-interest critics who believe Lincoln should have been more attentive to their favorite causes.)

As any individual would be, Lincoln was occasionally

irritated by the constant criticism and advice-giving he received from all sides. To one group demanding something or other he compared himself to the tightrope walker Blondin, who once walked across Niagara Falls on a tightrope with a man on his back and who performed many other fantastic feats before open-mouthed crowds in Europe and America. "Gentlemen," he said to these supplicants, "suppose all the property you are worth was in gold, and you had put it into the hands of Blondin to carry across the Niagara River on a tight-rope. Would you shake the cable, or keep shouting out to him, 'Blondin, stand up a little straighter!' 'Blondin, stoop a little more!' 'Blondin, go a little faster!' 'Lean a little more to the north!' 'Bend over a little more to the south!' No, gentlemen, you would hold your breath as well as your tongues, and keep your hands off until he was over. The government is carrying an immense weight. Untold treasures are in their hands. They are doing the very best they can. Do not badger them. Keep silence, and we will get you safe across."

Of course Lincoln did not expect his critics to keep silent, and they did not. But he kept his balance, anyway, and got safely across with the whole nation on his back.

Lincoln's position in the no-man's-land between sections at war and between competing factions within the North demanded a virtuoso performance in balanced political leadership. And Lincoln came through. He had the required firmness, adaptability, patience, and vision. Walt Whitman saw him as a classic figure in one of the world's classic dramas. "As I dwell on what I myself heard or saw of the mighty Westerner," wrote Whitman after the war, "and blend it with the history and literature of my age, and of what I can get of all ages, and conclude it with his death, it seems like some tragic play, superior to all else I know—vaster and fierier and more convulsionary for this America of ours than Aeschylus and Shakespeare ever drew for Athens or for England."

Perhaps the best and briefest appreciation of Lincoln as a war leader came from the pen of a man who had been a lieutenant-general in the Confederate Army. Concluding a paragraph of memoirs in which he eulogized Robert E. Lee, James Longstreet wrote, "Without doubt the greatest man of rebellion times, the one matchless among forty millions . . . was Abraham Lincoln."

Notes

Prologue

Three versions of Lincoln's farewell remarks are in his *Collected Works*, ed. Roy P. Basler (1953), 4:190–91. Hereafter cited as *CW*.

1. Lincoln's Youth

"They looked more human," Emanuel Hertz, *The Hidden Lincoln* (1938), 350; Lincoln was "diligent for knowledge," ibid.; "proved a good and kind mother," *CW*, 4:62; "If slavery is not wrong . . . ," *CW*, 7:281.

2. The New Salem Years

Education "the most important subject," *CW*, 1:8; Fought "a good many bloody struggles with the musquetoes [*sic*]," ibid., 510.

3. Springfield and the Law

"Well, Speed, I'm moved," William H. Herndon and Jesse W. Weik, *Herndon's Life of Lincoln* (1961 ed.), 171; Lincoln was "deficient in those little links," ibid.; "I most emphatically . . . made a fool of myself," *CW*, 1:117–19; "Let it hang there undisturbed," Herndon and Weik, *Herndon's Lincoln*, 379–80; Lincoln's "countenance and all his features seemed to take part," ibid., 259; "there was a zest and bouquet about his stories," Henry Clay Whitney, *Life on the Circuit with Lincoln* (1940), 174; "I never saw so melancholy and gloomy a face," Albert J. Beveridge, *Abraham Lincoln 1809–1858* (1928), 1:208; "the saddest face I ever attempted to paint," F. B. Carpenter, *Anecdotes and Reminiscences of President Lincoln*, in Henry J. Raymond, *Life and Public Services of Abraham Lincoln* (1865), 726.

4. Marriage and Upward Mobility

Not "satisfied that his heart was going with his hand," Herndon and Weik, *Herndon's Lincoln*, 192; Lincoln as the "most miserable man living," *CW*, 1:229; "there is one still unhappy," ibid., 282, 289; "Are you . . . glad you are married?" ibid., 303; Speed's comment, "If I had not been married," Herndon and Weik, *Herndon's Lincoln*, 192; Lincoln calls self "a strange, friendless, uneducated, penniless boy," *CW*, 1:320; "being elected to Congress has not pleased me," ibid., 391; "The legitimate object of government . . . ," ibid., 2:221; on Polk as "bewildered, confounded," ibid., 431–42; Lincoln on Taylor: "I am satisfied we can elect him," ibid., 452; "almost sweating blood" for Taylor, ibid., 2:48–49.

5. The Spread of Slavery: The Republican Victory in 1860

The repeal of the Missouri Compromise "aroused him," *CW*, 4:67; "I hate it because of the monstrous injustice," ibid., 2:255; "I wish to make and to keep the distinction," ibid., 248; "The rail candidate," ibid., 4:48n., and Mark E. Neely, Jr., *The Abraham Lincoln Encyclopedia* (1982), 138; "I have said this so often already," *CW*, 4:132–33; "We have just carried an election," ibid., 172; "By no act or complicity of mine," Harry E. Pratt, *Concerning Mr. Lincoln* (1944), 42.

6. An Underestimated Westerner

"We must accept the results," Ralph Waldo Emerson, *Journals* (1913), 9:556; "I give up the United States," William Howard Russell, *My Diary North and South* (1965), 257; "I have come to see you," *CW*, 4:223; the Union "would not be anything like a regular marriage," ibid., 195; "I recollect thinking then," ibid., 235–36; the Declaration gave liberty "not alone to the people of this country," ibid., 240.

7. Disunion and the Outbreak of War

"Well, gentlemen, I have been wondering," *Conversations with Lincoln*, ed. Charles M. Segal (1961), 90; "In your hands, my dissatisfied fellow countrymen," *CW*, 4:271; "by combinations too powerful to be suppressed," ibid., 331–32; Jefferson Davis on Lincoln's "declaration of war," *Messages and Papers of Jefferson Davis and the Confederacy* (1966), 1:63; "Both parties deprecated war," *CW*, 8:332–33.

8. The North as Underdog

"No people ever warred for independence with more relative advantages," *Battles and Leaders of the Civil War* (1956), 1:222; "to maintain unimpaired and in full vigor the rights and sovereignty of the States," *Messages and Papers of the Presidents*, comp. James D. Richardson (1907), 3:299; "We have never been a nation," George Templeton Strong, *Diary* (1952), 3:109; "The fact is that our Union rests upon public opinion," *Messages and Papers of the Presidents*, 5:636; the struggle with the South "presents to the whole family of man . . . ," *CW*, 4:426.

9. War and Disaster in the East

"If we cannot beat the enemy where he now is," *CW,* 5:461; "If hell is worse," Rutherford B. Hayes, *Diary and Letters* (1922–26), 3:627; "greater efforts to drive from our soil," John Hay, *Lincoln and the Civil War in the Diaries and Letters of John Hay* (1972), 67, emphasis added; "We had them within our grasp," ibid.; "What does it mean, Mr. Welles?" Gideon Welles, *Diary* (1960), 1:370.

10. War and Progress in the West: Ulysses S. Grant

"I gave up all idea of saving the Union," U. S. Grant, *Memoirs* (1885), 1:368; "The particulars of your plans," *CW,* 7:324.

11. Life in the White House

"I think nothing equals Macbeth . . . ," *CW,* 6:392; "Flub dubs for that damned old house," Benjamin Brown French, *A Yankee's Journal* (1989), 382; "What will Miss Harris think?" *Mary Todd Lincoln: Her Life and Letters,* 222; "She won't think any thing about it," ibid.; "The President is the best of us," Earl Conrad, *The Man Who Would Be President* (1961), 404; "Not everyone knows, as I do," Hay to Stanton, July 26, 1865, Stanton Papers, Library of Congress; "My husband and himself were very warmly attached," Mary Todd Lincoln to Sally Orne, Dec. 29, 1869, *Life and Letters,* 538.

12. Northern Discord over Slavery

"They are just what we would be," *CW,* 2:255; "the first and most powerful is slavery," Frederick Douglass, "Address to the People of the United States," in *A Documentary History of the Negro People,* ed. Herbert Aptheker (1951), 1:516; "All knew that . . . [slavery] was, somehow, the cause of the war," *CW*, 8:332; "Neither confiscation . . . or forcible abolition of slavery should be contemplated," the *Civil War Papers of George B. McClellan*, ed. Stephen W. Sears (1989), 344–45; "We think you are unduly influenced," *N. Y. Tribune*, Aug. 20, 1862; "My paramount object in this struggle *is* to save the Union," *CW*, 5:388–89.

13. Emancipation

"I have no purpose directly or indirectly," *CW*, 4:263; "as a fit and necessary war measure," ibid., 6:28–31; "an ineffaceable disgrace," Camilla A. Quinn, *Lincoln's Springfield in the Civil War* (1991), 41–42; "almost impossible for me to retain my commission," *Civil War Papers of George B. McClellan*, 481; "to the extent of his limited ability," Roy Franklin Nichols, *Franklin Pierce* (1931), 521; "the most execrable measure," *Messages and Papers of Jefferson Davis and the Confederacy*, 1:290; "a mongrel concern of whites, negroes, mulattoes, and sambos," Joseph George, Jr., "'Abraham Africanus I': President Lincoln through the Eyes of a Copperhead Editor," *Civil War History* 14, no. 3 (Sept. 1968): 232; "The war is and will be carried on," *CW*, 7:507.

14. Hostility in the North for Lincoln and His War

"Any disloyal practice affording aid and comfort to Rebels," *CW*, 5:436–37; "Every person in favor of Free Speech . . . ," *New York Weekly Caucasian*, April 18, 1863; "Which do we prefer," Joseph George, Jr., "'A Catholic Family Newspaper' Views the Lincoln Administration," *Civil War History* 24, no. 2 (June 1978): 124; "Time will but burn," *Union Pamphlets of the Civil War*, ed. Frank Freidel (1967), 2:731–32; "I am a Democrat," Frank L. Klement, *Limits of*

Dissent (1970), 162–63; "in time of war the mere arbitrary will of the President," Horace Greeley, *The American Conflict* (1866), 2:477–78; "Let us . . . keep cool," *CW,* 7:497–98; "The Confederacy is more formidable," Frank Everson Vandiver, *Jubal's Raid* (1960), 174; "Our only hope," Anna Ridgely, "A Girl in the Sixties," *Journal of the Illinois State Historical Society* 22, no. 3 (Oct. 1929): 438.

15. Reelection in 1864

"It will be my duty," *CW,* 7:514; "It has demonstrated," ibid., 8:100–101.

16. The Anti-Lincoln Reaction: John Wilkes Booth

"That means nigger citizenship," *House Report* 7, 40 Cong., 1 sess., 1867, 674.

17. April 14, 1865

"Tell mother I die for my country," *Assassination of President Lincoln and the Trial of the Conspirators,* comp. Benn Pitman (facsimile ed., 1954), 93.

18. Democracy's Martyr

"the happiness and value of life to all people of all colors everywhere, *CW,* 2:406.

19. Lincoln the War Leader

"I claim not to have controlled events . . . ," *CW,* 7:282; Lincoln "has shown . . . an almost supernatural tact," *Walt Whitman's Civil War,* ed. Walter Lowenfels (1960), 174–75;

"stood in the presence of the great guiding intellect," *CW,* 7:507; "He mastered and directed public sentiment," *Our Martyr President* (1865), 154–55; "Mr. Lincoln has exerted a greater influence," Isaac Arnold, *Cong. Globe,* Jan. 6, 1864, 117; "Public opinion in this country," *CW,* 3:424; "Any policy to be permanent," ibid., 4:9; "I have found in the course of long experience," James M. McPherson, "How Lincoln Won the War with Metaphors," *Eighth Annual R. Gerald McMurtry Lecture* (1985), 7; "trying with all his might to understand," Russell, *My Diary,* 256; "Intelligent understanding" a chief characteristic, Charles A. Dana, *Recollections of the Civil War* (1963), 159; "It is my duty to hear all," *CW,* 6:504; "The Tycoon is in fine whack," Hay, *Diaries and Letters,* 76; "The old man sits here . . . like a backwoods Jupiter," ibid., 91; "I believe he will fill a bigger place in history," to Charles G. Halpine, Aug. 14, 1863, Halpine Papers, Huntington Library, San Marino, Calif.; "I hope to stand firm enough," *CW,* 7:24; "if both factions, or neither, shall abuse you," ibid., 6:234; "Gentlemen, suppose all the property you are worth," F. B. Carpenter, *Six Months in the White House* (1867), 257–58; "As I dwell on what I myself heard or saw of the mighty Westerner," *Walt Whitman's Civil War,* 261; "Without doubt the greatest man of rebellion times," *Battles and Leaders of the Civil War,* 2:405.

Bibliographical Essay

References

The single most important source for the study of Lincoln is *The Collected Works of Abraham Lincoln*, ed. Roy P. Basler (1953), 9 vols., plus supplements in 1974 and 1987. Two indispensable references are Mark E. Neely, Jr., *The Abraham Lincoln Encyclopedia* (1982) and *Lincoln Day by Day: A Chronology*, Earl Schenck Miers, editor-in-chief (1960), 3 vols. Mabel Kunkel's *Abraham Lincoln: Unforgettable American* (1976) is a large and useful compendium of Lincoln sites, memorials, collections, and miscellany.

Biographies

The best of the traditional biographies published in the second half of the twentieth century are Benjamin P. Thomas, *Abraham Lincoln* (1952); Carl Sandburg, *Abraham Lincoln: The Prairie Years and the War Years* (1954, a one-volume edition far superior to the original six-volume edition); and Stephen B. Oates, *With Malice toward None* (1977). Charles B. Strozier's *Lincoln's Quest for Union* (1982) contains original insights into Lincoln's character and motivation.

There are innumerable other biographies, but for the prepresidential years William H. Herndon and Jesse W. Weik's *Herndon's Life of Lincoln* (1961 ed.) and Albert J. Beveridge's *Abraham Lincoln 1809–1858* (1928), 2 vols., are especially important. For the presidential years, so are John G. Nicolay and John Hay's *Abraham Lincoln: A History* (1890), 10 vols., and James G. Randall's *Lincoln the President* (1945–55), 4 vols.

Mark E. Neely, Jr., has recently published *The Last Best Hope of Earth: Abraham Lincoln and the Promise of America*, a succinct and informed analysis of Lincoln's presidency. Several other Lincoln scholars, David Donald among them, are at work on full-scale biographies that may be expected in the near future.

Collections of Lincoln photographs, including friends and relatives, are Charles Hamilton and Lloyd Ostendorf, *Lincoln in Photographs* (Morningside ed., 1985); Philip B. Kunhardt, Jr., Richard Kunhardt III, and Peter W. Kunhardt, *Lincoln: An Illustrated Biography* (1992); and James Mellon, *The Face of Lincoln* (1979). Americans who lived during his lifetime were more familiar with Lincoln's looks through the work of engravers and lithographers than that of photographers. See Harold Holzer, Gabor S. Boritt, and Mark E. Neely, Jr., *The Lincoln Image* (1984) and *Improving the Lincoln Image* (1985).

Important biographical material can be found in books dealing with Lincoln's wife and family: Jean H. Baker, *Mary Todd Lincoln* (1987); *Mary Todd Lincoln: Her Life and Letters*, ed. Justin G. Turner and Linda Levitt Turner (1972); and Mark E. Neely, Jr., and R. Gerald McMurtry, *The Insanity File: The Case of Mary Todd Lincoln* (1986).

Several periodicals are devoted exclusively to the study of Lincoln. Listed here alphabetically with years and frequency of publication in parentheses, they are the *Abraham Lincoln Quarterly* (1940–52); the *Journal of the Abraham Lincoln Association* (1979 to present; 1979–86 called *Papers of ALA*; now published semi-annually); the *Lincoln Herald* (1929 to present, quarterly); and *Lincoln Lore* (1928 to present, monthly). Each issue of the *Lincoln Herald* contains a comprehensive "Lincoln News Digest" reporting Lincoln-related activities, conferences, speeches, and articles that have taken place during the quarter. Such matters are also reported annually in the *Journal of the Abraham Lincoln Association*, together with an exhaustive summary of all scholarly and popular productions in the field of Lincolniana.

The *Journal of Illinois History* carries many articles relating to Lincoln, especially in its spring issue. Those written by James T. Hickey are available in his *Collected Writings* (1990). *Civil War History* publishes important Lincoln articles, as do many other scholarly and general-interest journals.

Among the most significant books of essays published by leading Lincoln scholars and dealing with various phases of Lincoln's life are David Donald, *Lincoln Reconsidered* (1947); Richard N. Current, *The Lincoln Nobody Knows* (1958); and Don Fehrenbacher, *Lincoln in Text and Context* (1987).

Lincoln to 1861

Louis A. Warren's *Lincoln's Youth* (1959) draws a more favorable picture of Lincoln's early life than do Herndon and Beveridge, above. Don Davenport's *In Lincoln's Footsteps* (1991) is an interesting traveler's guide to the places in Illinois, Indiana, and Kentucky where Lincoln visited or lived. The breach between Lincoln and his father is considered in John Y. Simon's "House Divided: Lincoln and His Father," *Tenth Annual R. Gerald McMurty Lecture* (1987).

Benjamin P. Thomas in *Lincoln's New Salem* (1934) describes what life was like for Lincoln after he moved into the small village as an adult. Recent views of Ann Rutledge are John Y. Simon, "Abraham Lincoln and Ann Rutledge, *Journal of the Abraham Lincoln Association* 2 (1990); John Evangelist Walsh, *The Shadows Rise* (1993); and Douglas Wilson, "Abraham Lincoln and Ann Rutledge," *Civil War History* 38, no. 4 (Dec. 1990). The town of Vandalia when Lincoln lived in it is described by William E. Baringer in *Lincoln's Vandalia* (1949) and

Mary Burtschi in *Vandalia: Wilderness Capital* (1963). Paul Angle describes the city in which Lincoln spent most of his adult life, Springfield, Illinois, in *Here I Have Lived* (1935). P. M. Zall's *Abe Lincoln Laughing* (1982) is the most scholarly collection of numerous anecdotes by and about Lincoln.

Paul Simon in *Lincoln's Preparation for Greatness* (1971) analyzes Lincoln's legislative experience, and Gabor S. Boritt in *Lincoln and the Economics of the American Dream* (1978) demonstrates Lincoln's lifelong commitment to the use of government, where necessary, so that all people might have a chance to better their lots in life. In "Abraham Lincoln and 'That Fatal First of January,'" *Civil War History* 38, no. 2 (June 1992), Douglas L. Wilson speculates about the broken engagement to Mary Todd. John J. Duff in *A. Lincoln: Prairie Lawyer* (1960) approaches the law practice from a biographical point of view, while John P. Frank in *Lincoln as a Lawyer* (1961) treats it more technically. Paul Findley gives an account of Lincoln's single term in Congress in *A. Lincoln: The Crucible of Congress* (1979).

The profound influence of the Kansas-Nebraska Act on Lincoln is well described by Don E. Fehrenbacher in *Prelude to Greatness* (1962) and Allan Nevins in *The Emergence of Lincoln* (1950–51), 2 vols. In the *Lincoln-Douglas Debates: The First Complete and Unexpurgated Text* (1993), editor Harold Holzer presents the text of each debater's speeches as they were published in newspapers friendly to his rival. David Potter's *The Impending Crisis* (1976) gives a revealing analysis of the vote in the presidential election of 1860.

Lincoln, 1861–65

The issue of how the war actually began is thoroughly examined by Richard N. Current in *Lincoln and the First Shot* (1963). The best one-volume study of the Civil War is James McPherson, *Battle Cry of Freedom* (1988), and an important advantage of Allan Nevins's *The War for the Union* (1959–71), 4 vols., over other multivolume histories is that it does not neglect politics and the home front. As commander-in-chief, Lincoln is given high marks by Trevor Nevitt Dupuy in *The Military Life of Abraham Lincoln* (1969), by Colin R. Ballard in *The Military Genius of Abraham Lincoln* (1952), and by T. Harry Williams in *Lincoln and His Generals* (1952).

For Northern prejudice against blacks, see Leon Litwack, *North of Slavery* (1961), and Jacque Voegeli, *Free but Not Equal* (1967). In *Lincoln and Black Freedom* (1981), LaWanda Cox shows how sensitive Lincoln was to the problem of white prejudice. John Hope Franklin's *The Emancipation Proclamation* (1963) is a brief summary.

That there was substantial hostility for Lincoln and his war in his own hometown is established by Camilla A. Quinn in *Lincoln's Springfield in the Civil War* (1991). In *The Copperheads in the Middle West* (1960) and the *Limits of Dissent* (1970), Frank L. Klement argues that the Copperhead menace was not so real as Republicans asserted. The opposite point of view is convincingly given by G. R. Tredway in *Democratic Opposition to the Lincoln Administration in Indiana* (1973). In *The Fate of Liberty* (1991), Mark E. Neely, Jr., makes the first detailed analysis of military arrests of civilians.

The presidential election of 1864 was perhaps the most critical in American history, but it lacks a scholarly monograph. David E. Long is working on one and has published "The Race Issue in the 1864 Election" in *Lincoln Herald* (Winter 1992; Spring 1993; Summer 1993). William Frank Zornow has written "Treason as a Campaign Issue in the Reelection of Lincoln," *Abraham Lincoln Quarterly* 5, no. 6 (June 1949), as well as a book overstressing divisions within the Republican party: *Lincoln and the Party Divided* (1954).

That Confederate officers were interested in a plan to capture Lincoln very similar to the one John Wilkes Booth sought to execute is shown by John C. Brennan in "General Bradley

T. Johnson's Plan to Abduct President Lincoln," *Chronicles of St. Mary's* (Nov. and Dec. 1974). For more on Booth, see Asia Booth Clarke, *The Unlocked Book: A Memoir . . . by His Sister* (1938); Stanley Kimmel, *The Mad Booths of Maryland,* 2d ed. (1969); and Gene Smith, *American Gothic* (1992).

The principal myth that George S. Bryan seeks to dispel in his judicious *The Great American Myth* (reprint ed., 1990) is that Booth escaped and the War Department covered up the fact. In *The Lincoln Murder Conspiracies* (1983) William Hanchett treats the assassination as an act of war and refutes many conspiratorial theories, especially the one that involves Secretary Stanton and the War Department.

An informed descriptive account of the assassination and of Booth's attempt to escape is by Michael W. Kauffman, "John Wilkes Booth and the Murder of Abraham Lincoln, *Blue and Gray Magazine* (Apr. and June 1990). W. Emerson Reck has written *A. Lincoln: His Last 24 Hours* (1987). The very first assumption about the assassination—that it was a Rebel/Copperhead plot—is given scholarly revival by William A. Tidwell with James O. Hall and David Winfred Gaddy in *Come Retribution* (1988).

For the impact of the assassination on the American people, see Thomas Reed Turner, *Beware the People Weeping* (1992); Lloyd Lewis, *Myths after Lincoln* (1941 ed.); Victor Searcher, *The Farewell to Lincoln* (1965); and Dorothey Meserve Kunhardt and Philip B. Kunhardt, Jr., *Twenty Days* (1965).

Lincoln's ceaseless efforts to amass new weaponry to defeat the South is shown in Robert V. Bruce, *Lincoln and the Tools of War* (1989). James McPherson in "How Lincoln Won the War with Metaphors," *Eighth Annual R. Gerald McMurty Lecture* (1989), stresses Lincoln's ability to communicate with the people. In *Lincoln the War President,* ed. Gabor S. Boritt (1992), leading scholars give much by-no-means uncritical credit to Lincoln for the North's victory.

Index

WILLIAM HANCHETT, professor of history emeritus at San Diego State University, is the author of *Irish: Charles G. Halpine in Civil War America*, of *The Lincoln Murder Conspiracies*, and of many articles on Lincoln and the Civil War era. In addition to writing the script for the video version of this book, he has written the script for the video documentary "Black Easter: The Assassination of Abraham Lincoln."